SLAVES OF THE WAR LORDS

SLAVES OF THE WAR LORDS

by

HENRY RUSSELL

(10th Bn Worcesters)

57 Bde/19 (Western) Division

10th R. Warwicks
8th Gloucesters
10th Worcesters
8th N. Staffs

HUTCHINSON & CO. (Publishers) LTD.
34-36 Paternoster Row, LONDON E.C.4

CONTENTS

SLAVES OF THE WAR LORDS

CHAPTER I

THE DRAFT

PHOENIX PARK, DUBLIN, the 2nd of September, 1916. A double line of men were standing to attention between the rows of tents. Officers by the dozen and privates by the score were grouped on either side watching the scene with interest.

The polished bugles of the band were raised in readiness.

Words of command, sharp and crisp, echoed through the camp.

"Form-fours!"

"Right!"

"By the left—quick—march!"

The drums rolled; the bugles began the first notes of a march; the men swung into step, and the draft was off. Instantly discipline and prudence was cast to the winds. Soldiers ran alongside the marching column, shaking hands with comrades whom the gods of war had called, wishing them luck and a safe return.

Through the park; through the crowded city and so to the docks and the boat.

There on the quay stood the divisional General and

his staff, and the divisional band, and hosts of soldiers, officers and men mingling together to catch the last glimpse, to give the last cheer.

Up the rigging of adjacent ships they swarmed, and as the troopship moved slowly away, the General waved his hand, the band played stirring music, and cheer after cheer rang out, sustained until the coastline had faded into the horizon. Thus ended the glamour of war.

The scene had thrilled me—would have thrilled anyone. It was the sweets of war, sweets which already contained their quota of bitterness. We had been refused embarkation leave. Our need over there was too great, they had said.

A last look at the old home; a last handshake, painful though it might have been, would have made the going easier. I looked at the men around me; some seemed happy and carefree, others thoughtful and quiet. Citizens of a few months ago; soldiers of the present; what of the future? So many to die; so many to be maimed; so many to return. If only they knew. If only I knew. Gladly would I have torn aside the veil which screened the secrets of the coming months and years. I would, I thought, be content, if only I knew. My mind wandered over the events which had brought me there; of the first mad impulse that made me join the surging throng of enthusiasts who clamoured to enlist, and the coldness of those wet blankets; the doctors, who raised the parrot cry "Too small, too small." How I had cursed my physique. How I had trained in my own way until I had felt fitter than I had ever done, and still the cry was "Too small, too small."

THE DRAFT

So I had left it at that and the war progressed and men died in ever-increasing numbers, and live men brought home harrowing tales of war, and recruiting was dwindling despite newspaper stunts and widespread propaganda.

Came the time when desperate measures were imminent and Lord Derby on the peak of another wave of patriotism roped in a cool hundred thousand, and roped me in with them, for the cry was no longer "Too small, too small."

My knowledge of war was limited, my craving for war was nil. I did not want to stick any German. I did not want any German to stick me. I would have liked the war to finish before the French coast hove in sight.

The glamour of war was stirring, but what of the other side? In common with the majority, I had laughed over the Bairnsfather cartoons. I thought Old Bill looked screamingly funny standing in a hole with shells flying all around him, and asking Herb. where that one had gone. Old Bill was such an incorrigible optimist. He made war look like a holiday, only funnier. No. I did not like war, but I liked Old Bill, and the cheers and the band. I was so very ordinary.

The sea was smooth; the air was warm. It was quite comfortable lying on the deck with the pack for a pillow. Perhaps war was not so bad after all. Men, and especially soldiers, do exaggerate.

Holyhead, and trains ready waiting. It was getting dark. It would be too dark to see familiar places.

The midlands, the home of the draft. Why was the train speeding up so?

"They think we might do a guy," says a fellow, with a wry smile. Was it really speeding up, or did we object to any speed? Minds can become so biased at times.

"I'd jump here if the perishin' train would slow up," said another. So through the night we travelled and early next morning reached Folkestone. Military police sprang up like mushrooms; they watched us left and right; they brought up the rear; they took infinite care that no man should wander hapless or forlorn, and they escorted us to a street of one-time boarding-houses now under military occupation.

Splendid houses, splendid billets, and a splendid view, but barbed wire and sentries marred the scene. Barbed wire to discourage the good people of Folkestone from hero-worship. Not it. Folkestone was war sick and these were elementary precautions to keep together the timid and the wayward. England's potential fighters must take their farewell of the homeland as prisoners of the War Lords.

We rested for a few hours and were given food and, directly after midday, we started for the boat.

I looked for excitement; there was none. A few people watched with the same casual interest that a railway porter watches the departure of a half-day excursion. A couple of flappers giggled at the sentry by the wire and several dogs chased through the compound.

"Get a move on there," cried the guardian angels with red caps.

"Who the hell yer pushing. Boat can wait, can't it," yelled a private as he stepped on the gangway.

THE DRAFT

"Got a cushy billet, ain't you, mate," sounded from behind.

"Afore you come up, chum, at Mons, and don't forget," retorted a redcap, with emphasis on the "Mons".

We crowded to the sides of the boat and remained there until the chalk cliffs of England had disappeared from our view.

Boulogne seemed to be a confused medley of masts and shipping. Boats moored to the docks, boats anchored further afield. Boats being unloaded of their cargoes of war material; French submarines and destroyers, bluejackets and fishermen, but khaki always predominant. Boulogne was being Anglicized. Small children greeted us with English words. Some clamoured for us to purchase "Buisceets—choc-o-late—spearmint," but the older people were not even curious. The continual passing of troops had deadened their interest, with the exception of those who for mercenary reasons welcomed them in any number and at any time.

That night I slept under canvas at the top of St. Martin's Hill. The tents were camouflaged with red paint.

"Looks like blood, chum," said an unsophisticated private to one of the camp staff.

"Looks like it? It is it. Them's what they carried the wounded on at Loos," replied the man with a grin.

We moved by train to Calais, and for three weeks divided our time by drilling and unloading boats at the docks. Three weeks, and we had been refused embarkation leave. Our need over here was too great, they had said. On the "bull-ring", where we received the finishing touches of our training, very little gaiety or peace of mind was to be found. The drill instructors were a tough lot and believed in hardening men, and they certainly enjoyed themselves during the process.

Their especial vogue was bayonet fighting, and armed with a pole on the end of which was fastened some soft material they would select some unfortunate private and jab the pole in his face or chest.

"Come on now, get at me; kill me; jab, man, jab. You're not handlin' the old woman's umbrella. You're as good as dead afore you start. You won't last ten seconds against a decent Jerry. Lord, fancy sending you over here."

It would be the duty of the man to attack the instructor with rifle and bayonet, properly sheathed, of course, and after some minutes' horseplay, the instructor would unexpectedly fall on another, and repeat the performance.

Another diversion which was the source of much amusement to the base staff, was the running of men wearing gas masks until they were scarcely able to breathe, and more than one man collapsed as a result of this punishing exercise.

We heard much of that mystic phrase "up the line". Nearby was an important railway, and many freight trains would daily steam away. We would watch them out of sight and be thrilled to think that they were travelling towards the line. Men would be pointed out who had spent months in the trenches, and we looked upon them with awe and reverence and accorded them the respect due to such veterans.

The food which was served out was both good and

bad. We messed in tents and rations were drawn for each tent. This included butter in tins, biscuits, bread, and the inevitable jam. Dinner was usually a concoction of greasy, evil-looking stew which we invariably managed to do without. French women sold bread and other eatables from stalls near the camp, and it was always possible, providing one had the money, to supplement rations from this source. Off-duty hours were spent in various ways. There was a substantial canteen, a Y.M.C.A. hut, and a crowd of "House" gamesters. Cries of "Kelly's eye", "clickety click", and "legs eleven" resounded from all parts of the camp. It was the only game of a gambling nature officially approved by the authorities, but not the only game which was played. The proprietor of the "Crown and Anchor" sheet could always be found in odd nooks and corners inviting all and sundry to have a little bit on the old "mudhook".

One well-remembered day the draft was paraded and informed that henceforth they would be known as Worcesters, for the whole of us had been detailed to a battalion of that famous line regiment, and not long afterwards we found ourselves in a troop-train heading in that direction which had for some time so whetted our curiosity.

CHAPTER II

TO THE LINE

MY first impression of soldiers "resting" was none too nice. It was a warm day. We came to some farm buildings, and in the fields sat scores of "Tommies" clad in trousers and boots. They were handling under-garments and industriously studying them.

I shuddered.

"Dirty beasts," I thought. "Fancy getting in that condition."

We halted near to a couple of men. One held up his shirt and grinned.

"Got any, chum," said he. "You'll soon have some if you haven't."

"Not if I can help it," I replied in my ignorance. I did not know then that they were the clean men who took off their shirts at every opportunity.

He noticed the disgust written on the faces of the draft. He nudged his companion and they both laughed.

"Wait for a month or two and you'll be doing the same, that's if you want any sleep at nights."

We were dismissed and assigned to quarters. Mine was a straw-covered barn filled with men who were consuming large chunks of French bread, and jam.

Evidently the issue bread had run short. It had, they told me. Five in a loaf and lucky to get that.

A pleasant-faced private made room for me, and I took off my equipment and sat down, thankful for a rest.

"Just come out, chum?" he asked.

"Yes," I replied, taking stock of my surroundings. "Seems pretty full up in here."

"About the usual," he replied. "We never get overmuch room. Just enough to lie down and turn round. Got any bread and 'possie'?"

I unfastened my haversack and produced, in army parlance, the unconsumed portion of the day's ration, a slice of bread and a half-empty tin of bully.

"No possie," he said again. "Here, try this, it's poor stuff. Australian quince, but it 'tices the bread down."

Somehow I enjoyed that meal. Afterwards I learnt much from my genial colleague. They had recently come from the Somme where terrible casualties had been incurred. The draft was to fill the gaps. How long they were out for they did not know. Most likely a fortnight, but perhaps longer.

"It was hell down there," he confided. "I don't want to see the Somme again in a hurry. I'd rather put a bullet through my arm than suffer that lot again."

"That would get you into a tidy bother," I suggested.

"Oh, it can be worked," he replied. "I know one or two who have got away with it; a wet sandbag, nicely folded, stops the burn."

"What burn," I inquired.

"Well, you are an innocent," he said. "A bullet from close range burns the flesh round the wound and they've got you in a tick, and it's a certain two years when you are better. That's what the sandbag's for, compree."

He took me around the billets. The barns and sheds were attached to the farmhouse forming three sides of a square. The fourth was made up by a private roadway or mud-track according to the state of the weather.

In the centre of the square was the proverbial muck-heap common to most French farms that I afterwards visited. An offensive stench came from the muck-heap, and a crowd of ducks occupied the one portion which contained stagnant water. Why these dung-heaps were tolerated I have never discovered. They were breeding-places for flies, and flies carry disease, but no self-respecting rural farmer would allow it to be interfered with.

I remember one officer who held strong views of cleanliness, and he ordered a fatigue-party to clear up a particularly obnoxious dung-heap. Immediately the whole of the household were gesticulating and shouting and harassing the officer, and finally he called off the fatigue-party and allowed the dung-heap to fester undisturbed.

That night I wrote home, in the course of which I stated, "We have joined the Worcesters. They seem a decent lot of fellows, but not so gay and light-hearted as the papers lead us to believe. Recent experiences have evidently undermined their gaiety. Our chaps will have to cheer them up."

And to cheer them up we did our best.

On route-marches we sang with gusto the songs we had learned in England and Ireland.

"I wonder how long they will yell like that," said a gaunt-looking man with a scar running from ear to nose. The days passed quickly but not unpleasantly. The men were, on the whole, distinctly chummy, and the officer to whose platoon I had been attached was kindly considerate. He was interested in his platoon and proved it by supplementing the rations, when they were scarce, out of his own pocket. He believed in treating men like men and received in return the whole-hearted devotion of those under him. Not so the platoon sergeant, who was one of the old school. He detested any attempt to fraternize between officers and privates, and he would wait until the officer was out of sight and then prove his annoyance by introducing all the exercises and movements which were most tiring and which he knew we most detested.

"Some of you must think you're in a blooming nursery, the way he coddles yer," he would begin. "Don't think I'm going to be a wet nurse for yer. Double mark time! Forward, about turn! You come here—about turn!—to learn to fight—about turn!—not to be petted and spoilt—about turn!—by officers who don't know how to treat yer. Halt!"

If that sergeant could have received all that the platoon wished him to receive his subsequent army career would have depended on the skill of the hospital surgeons.

Rumours were the bane of our life. Each day added to the crop. "We're going back on the Somme." "We're for Ypres, Armentières, Egypt." "We're going back to England to give exhibition training."

Every man knew positively. Had heard it from a reliable source.

I attach some credence to a story told by an officer who said he was the only man who had tracked an army rumour to its source. This particular officer had been out of the trenches but a few hours and was in the position to know that a month's rest was practically certain. Then he heard that it was general knowledge among the troops that they were going in the line again. After much questioning he received the startling information that the news had come from his own batman, who in turn had got it from himself. Quickly he called the offending batman before him.

"Brown," he said, deliberately. "You started this rumour about going back up the line."

"I, sir?" said Brown. "Why, I've had dozens of chaps telling me that it was true."

"Perhaps so," the officer said. "But you started it and it's gone round and round and then back to you as a matter of course. Now what have you heard me say?"

Brown, cornered, had to make a confession.

"It's like this, sir. Just as I came in here yesterday I overheard you telling Lieutenant Smith that the old man, meaning the colonel, said that we were going up the line."

The captain thought for a few seconds.

"You damn fool," he said sternly. "What I said was that the old man, meaning the colonel, was on a line. Clear out. Any more of this and you will be returned to duty."

And so do rumours prosper and grow, and in their

travels rob the men of that peace of mind which is their greatest need while resting.

All too soon, the day came that we were paraded outside billets, and after the customary inspection marched to Bailleul. There we entrained in cattle trucks labelled "8 *chevaux*, 40 *hommes*", and proceeded to an unknown destination.

I thought this troop train was rather amusing. It would stop at the most unexpected times and start seemingly when it liked. Then for a couple of miles it would race along at a rattling pace, stop for five minutes, and then crawl for half a mile or so.

At these desultory halts men would get out to stretch their legs and perhaps wander a few yards away. There would be a creak and a rattle and a wild scramble back into the trucks, no easy task, the last of them being pulled bodily into the moving train. This occurred on every occasion, the troops apparently enjoying some amusement from the thrills which it afforded.

After darkness had fallen the train finally halted and we found ourselves at the comparatively important town of Doullens. The men were not elated. Doullens spelt the Somme to those who knew, but I was not unduly worried with the prospect, for my knowledge of that region had been obtained from gossip and newspaper reports.

"They kill mules down here," said the man by my side.

We began a weary trek. It had been raining heavily and the roads were covered with pools of water which splashed our legs at every step. I was in pretty good condition, but when I saw men falling out and I heard that they were putting their packs on the limbers behind, I began to feel a strong desire to do likewise.

I stepped on one side and waited for the limbers to come up; then casting off my equipment I dumped it on an obliging vehicle and walked sedately behind.

For another hour we marched thus and then came to an abrupt halt. I discovered with horror that "D" Company had side-tracked to its billets and that I, together with several more innocents, had followed the limbers to the transport lines. It took me two hours to find the company, and when I eventually located them I discovered that I had been crimed for falling out of the ranks and I was for orderly room the next morning at nine o'clock. There, I was severely admonished and threatened with field punishment number one if ever I repeated the performance. It was the first and last time that I received such admonition.

The following day we marched to Authe, where for a week we did a certain amount of field training, and then on again, to Warloy. We were now getting close to the seat of war, and the booming of the guns could be plainly heard.

Warloy was undoubtedly a neat, quiet little village in normal times, but the mark of the war was upon it. Not in shattered houses but in the ceaseless march of troops through and through the village, and in the clatter of transport and of guns. In the company of others I found a cottage where we indulged in an orgy of eggs and chips.

Madame in charge was doing a thriving business in this commodity, and had perhaps already accumulated a useful nest-egg for the time when her husband and sons should return from the front. Eggs and chips could be procured almost anywhere. Whether it was a national diet before the war I know not, but it was almost a national industry about that time. An amazing feature to me was the coolness with which the troops made use of the villagers' homes. It seemed as though every house was open to them. A man would open the door, walk in, and ask for a cup of coffee with the same indifference that one would walk into a restaurant. The only explanation was that the selling of cups of coffee, *sans* sugar, *sans* milk was, like eggs and chips, a paying proposition, and therefore, providing the troops were prepared to buy coffee, they were content to let them sit there and drink it. Many pleasant hours have I spent in the houses, seated near the peculiar bowl-shaped stove, sipping coffee, and listening to the chatter of the women who in their native tongue jabbered at a speed which I have heard few English women equal. Warloy was one of the long string of villages which held the unenviable distinction of being just behind the lines. We stayed there one night only, and late the next day moved beyond the scene of civilization to the outskirts of Albert.

Bivouacs were erected on ground not a quarter of a mile from the famous city. I took the opportunity of visiting it, and found the place much the same as the many photographs which had been published. The fallen Madonna still retained its remarkable position. Whole streets were derelict and deserted, except for the military population, which was small. I saw in Albert the hideousness of war, the madness of a civilization that creates but to destroy.

The roar of the guns had become louder, and before

sunset developed into a drumfire which I immediately recognized as a barrage. We crowded to some high ground and watched the flashes, as of lightning, in the distance.

Along the road which skirted the camp passed endless columns of transport. Red Cross ambulances coming from the direction of the line were too numerous to be pleasant, and occasionally lorries crowded with the lesser wounded would clatter by. A convoy of German prisoners with a minimum of escort passed along, the poor wretches looking tired and weary, but betraying unmistakable signs of the pleasure which they must have felt, knowing full well that their part in the conflict was ended.

The sights were not inspiring, and I turned in with a mind filled with misgivings over thoughts of the morrow.

It was a chill October night and, with but one blanket each, it was impossible to get warm. Long before daylight half the camp was astir, warming themselves by wood-fires fed by the numerous shell-boxes which lay conveniently near.

At nine o'clock we paraded. The company quarter-masters produced from somewhere sundry bombs, Verey lights, and spades; and I was soon the unwilling possessor of two new Mills bombs—nicely painted red on the ends to show that they were alive—a spade, rather shop-soiled, and a bundle of six Verey lights.

What with this extra lumber and a full day's rations, in addition to full marching-order, I began to have serious doubts as to whether I should ever reach those trenches. We marched off in platoons at intervals of one hundred yards. The first platoon was thus nearly a mile away before the sixteenth made a start. This method was found very useful on roads which carried a heavy amount of traffic, and even more useful in reducing casualties, for it is only logical to presume that a battalion spread over a mile offers an infinitely less target than the same battalion marching in one column.

We left the road soon after passing Albert, and the journey over broken and shell-battered ground was both irksome and tiring. The incessant drumfire became more violent. Halts were frequent for no apparent reason, although, had we known it, the actual reason was because of the ebb and flow of the local battle then in progress. The very trenches we were to occupy were in the possession of the enemy until late in the afternoon.

We began to pass the guns. To us new-comers they were objects of curiosity until we discovered their nasty habit of discharging salvoes at the most unexpected times and thereby giving us chronic attacks of nerves.

First the heavies, and then the field-guns, here, there, and everywhere, literally hundreds of them, and still we plodded along. Groups of dirty unshaven men came by, and R.A.M.C. orderlies, carrying stretchers on which lay groaning wounded with white faces peering from under blankets. There was a hiss and a roar and a shell had burst a hundred yards away. The pace quickened immediately.

I began to feel uncommonly tired, and longed for the sight of those trenches where at least some kind of a rest could be obtained. Fortunately, the ground was dry and prevented slipping, for a firm foothold to tired men is something of a boon.

At long last, just as the sun had set and twilight was deepening, we reached Field trench, which was the communication to that sector. The flagging spirits of the draft were cheered as they stepped into the trench. Personally, I felt a thrill and something of pride to realize that I was actually walking in trenches which all the world talked about. I soon realized that it was not an easy-going task, for there were many holes to avoid and signalling wire was stretched across the trench in a position to half-strangle the unwary.

Here I discovered the blessing of being intermixed with old campaigners, for they continually passed down word of any likely obstacles.

"Mind that hole." "Wire above." "Step up." "Step down." "Keep to the right," and so on.

Even this could be overdone, for word would be passed along too quickly, with the consequence that the object was being sought for long before it was reached, and eventually tripped over. I found that this constant passing back of the location of pitfalls was a permanent feature of trench life, and it was an unwritten law for the leading man to immediately apprise his comrades behind of anything likely to cause a fall, although he must first find them by stumbling himself.

The trench was long, or appeared to be long, for its actual length as the crow flies was multiplied by the many twists and turnings which gave the major safety from shell-fire.

The pace became terrific and exhausting. Most of

the time I was running to keep in sight the man in front, for it had become quite dark, and I knew that if I came to a double trench I should have an even chance of taking the wrong one. Unpleasant crashes and bursts of flame became frequent. We were being shelled going in.

Faster, faster! I had the utmost difficulty in keeping contact with the shadow in front.

For God's sake, go steady!

My breath was coming in gasps; I was sweating profusely; I was painfully thirsty and, moreover, my equipment seemed to weigh a ton. Round traverse after traverse, stumbling and recovering, shouting at the men in front, cursing and panting, the mad rush gradually slowed down, and we halted. I heard that two companies had gone into the front line, Regina trench, and that we were even now in the support line, Hessian.

I released my equipment with utter relief and dragged out my water-bottle. Then from my pack I produced half a tin of jam and some bread, and enjoyed an impromptu meal.

CHAPTER III

SUPPORTS AND RESERVE

I WAS alone in a piece of trench about six yards in length. Around each corner I knew other men were stationed, but that traverse evidently belonged to me. It was rather different to what I had imagined: no trench-boards, no woodwork of any description, just cold earth, with sides sloping outwards. So this, then, was the line of which I had heard so much. It seemed fairly quiet. Ha! Machine-gun; I almost felt pleased as I recognized the various sounds I had expected to hear. The whine of bullets was interesting. The trench was deep, and I felt safe between those walls of earth. Pottering about, I found a hole excavated in the side. I was tired and, knowing nothing of trench routine, and in the absence of orders to the contrary, I lay down.

The hole was small and my legs protruded well into the trench, but it was comfortable after the exhausting march and I certainly dozed.

A series of violent explosions in the immediate vicinity caused me to open my eyes and take notice. Shells, I thought. They began to crash with ever-increasing fury, and pieces of flying metal buried themselves in the sides of the trench with dull uncomfortable thuds. I lay there, affected by something more than curiosity.

The scene was vivid: just like what I had pictured in my mind in happier moments. The whole neighbourhood was alive with fire. Sometimes a shell would burst near and partially blind me with its flash, and a rain of earth would fall on my extended legs. The acrid smell of powder made me sneeze. I felt safer lying there and, after all, I decided, this was just ordinary trench warfare. It must be like this the greater part of the time, and I should have to get used to it.

Happily, I did not realize that the trench was being subjected to a fierce barrage and that my position was dangerously like that of a moth hovering near the naked light of a candle.

"Pass the word for stretcher-bearers," came from the next traverse. That sounded serious. I could hardly believe that in such a short time somebody had been wounded or killed.

I passed the word, and then curled into that hole as far as I could, and became a bit worried over my legs which I could not tuck away.

Someone came rushing by and trod on my foot, then cursed, and was gone. I could hear shouts and cries not very far away. I wondered what was happening—I had not the slightest inclination to get out and see.

Then came a tremendous crash on my left, and a scream of terror, and a man dashed round, yelling:

"Bring a spade! Bring a spade!

Galvanized into life, I crawled out of the hole and mechanically took hold of the spade which I had carried. The trench had been blown in in the next traverse and men were digging feverishly.

I started to help and felt wonderfully better in doing so.

"Damn fools, some of you! hiding in funkholes when a strafe's on," said a corporal, as he vigorously applied a spade. "Now, mind his head! Here he comes! Come on, matey, you ain't dead yet."

We heaved him out, alive, but badly bruised and shaken, but after a rest and a certain amount of attention he recovered sufficiently to walk unaided down the trench.

With the approach of dawn came the order to "stand to". This meant that until day had fully broken we must man the fire-step. "Stand to" at dawn and dusk was a ritual on the Western Front, for it was at those times that most attacks took place. The shelling had moderated a little, but it was still unpleasantly heavy.

I began to hear accounts of men being killed and men being wounded and of some who had been buried by shells. The night's shelling was voted fearful. Several seasoned campaigners said they had never endured anything worse, and I began to feel decidedly alarmed.

As it gradually became light I looked about. The trench interested me at first. It was wider than I had thought and the sides were broken and irregular with much shelling. It looked easier to defend at the back than the front, and little wonder, considering that the Germans had only recently been pushed out, and that consequently the defence had had to be turned round. The large amout of enemy equipment, rifles, and overcoats which were lying about gave some idea of the haste with which they had finally abandoned their stronghold.

In common with the others I looked over the top. It was comparatively safe from rifle fire, for the German line was some hundreds of yards away and our own front line intervened. A scene of chaos and desolation confronted me. Barbed wire in jumbled masses, shell-holes edge to edge, dead bodies lying here and there and not the vestige of a living thing. I could distinguish the contour of the front line by a continuous ridge which had been formed by the earth thrown out when the trench was originally dug. Beyond that the ground fell away towards the village of Grandecourt which lay in the valley on the far side of the Ancre.

Directly after "stand down" work commenced, for many repairs were necessary as a result of the previous night's shelling. The parapet required strengthening and many loads of earth had to be moved from the bottom of the trench.

I had walked a couple of traverses away from my original position when a sergeant beckoned me to a dugout. A man was lying where he had fallen, partly down the steps. I immediately recognized the face of a fellow who had come out with the draft. He was dead, and one of his legs, horribly mutilated, overhung the top step.

"I want you to help bury this chap," said the sergeant.

A feeling of nausea overcame me. I was terrified. I wanted to run pell-mell from the gruesome sight. The mangled limb hypnotized me.

The sergeant pointed to another man.

"He'll give you a hand."

"Sergeant," I said. "I can't do that, just yet."

He looked me up and down with a certain amount of contempt.

"You aren't a blarsted coward, are you?" he said, abruptly.

"Nothing of the kind," I replied. "I'm new to this game. Give me a chance to get used to it."

He seemed to see the drift of my remark.

"The sooner you get used to this business the better," he said. "You'll see worse sights than this, let me tell you. Go and fall in with the ration party."

I very soon discovered that burying the dead was not the only uncongenial task in the trenches and that a ration party could be both exhausting and dangerous. Rations were usually brought to a point near to the trenches by a carrying party composed of details who had been left out of the line, or by limbers, if roads were passable and unobserved, and from there they were picked up by a carrying party from the trenches.

It was never a pleasant task, for two sandbags filled with rations or coke are rather awkward to manipulate at the best of times, but the worst fate which could befall one was to get laden with a couple of tins of water, for these left neither hand free, and many were the dodges employed to steer clear of this unwelcome burden.

Of course, on this occasion, being a greenhorn, I naturally found myself the possessor of a couple of Pratts' petrol tins, each with its full complement of two gallons of water. The return journey commenced.

After covering the first quarter of a mile I felt that I should like to put the cans down for a few seconds.

I was the only member of the draft on the ration party and the seasoned men were setting up a pace even quicker than that of the previous night. Another quarter of a mile and I was bringing up the rear. I felt that I must put those cans down whatever happened. I did, and in a couple of minutes realized that I had the trench and the war to myself so far as I could see. I was undismayed, and started off again with renewed strength. The rifle I had slung across my shoulders, and at every few yards the accursed thing would twist over and stick in the side of the trench. Then a salvo of shells would burst a hundred yards ahead and I would wait to see if any more would follow. They would, just behind me, and then there would be a rush with the cans until the danger zone was passed.

During a temporary halt I was attracted by something in the side of the trench. I scraped some of the soil away and disclosed a human skull. The trench-diggers had missed his grave by the merest chance.

With many rests and an occasional drink out of one of the cans I finally reached the company some two hours after the others, and I was on the point of returning to the traverse where I had spent the previous night when I was hailed by the sergeant who had detailed me for the ration party.

"Hi, you, just go and give those chaps a hand round the corner," he said.

I went in the direction indicated and saw a man, decapitated, lying in the bottom of the trench.

Two privates, obviously distressed, were standing by.

"Catch hold of one of his legs, mate," said one of them.

I clenched my teeth and decided there and then I would get used to it.

I grasped a leg and helped to lift the dripping body over a low part of the back of the trench. A few shovelfuls of earth were thrown over him, and at the edge of the shell-hole, which was his grave, was thrust a German rifle, muzzle downwards.

"Who is he?" I asked.

"Don't know," was the reply. "Sergeant's got the particulars, I suppose."

"What's the rifle for?" I queried.

"Oh, they'll put a cross there when it's safe enough."

"Before we leave this part?" I said.

"No fear," replied the man. "It's too damned hot round here to do the job properly. He'll have an unknown soldier's cross for a certainty. You see, it's like this, in some parts of the line, bodies are carried out and buried in the proper cemeteries, but here, on the Somme, you either have to leave 'em lying out or bury 'em the best way you can."

My education in matters of war was proceeding rapidly.

That night I went out on a working party.

It had been decided to dig a new trench in front of the line. We crept into "No Man's Land" and, each at his allotted part, commenced. So did the shelling.

During training at home we had often been told that we must learn to dig with feverish energy, but it was never taken properly to heart. We learned here. I never knew that mere man could get under the ground so quickly. I did not get tired, only anxious to get the exposed parts of my body under cover. The shelling was heavy and sustained. Occasionally a man would utter a cry and hobble away towards the line.

"Lucky devil," a perspiring private, digging furiously, would murmur.

With a huge crash a shell exploded a few yards from me. The fellow digging just behind began to utter strange unintelligible sounds and with his fingers tried to tear away the earth. He attracted the attention of an officer, who ordered him to be led away. It was my first experience of shell-shock, that terrible affliction of the nerves from which so many men suffered.

Deeper and wider became the trench, and well within the allotted time it was completed and we were withdrawn. It commenced to rain and I found sanctuary on the steps of a dugout. Each step was occupied by tired men who dozed away the night. It was chilly and damp, and the air was thick from the smoke of many cigarettes. I became cramped and my legs ached, for it was impossible to move without raising a chorus of grunts from those nearest.

At dawn, when we stood to, the trench was a quagmire and it was still raining heavily. The shelling was hideous and life seemed one horrible nightmare.

The soft bed of the trench quickly became a foot deep in sticky clinging mud, and I found that the strain of withdrawing each foot was the hardest of tasks. Breakfast was taken, but mud was on the bread and each mouthful had its share of grit.

Some of the old hands boiled cans of water on

candles bound with strips of sandbagging, one candle sufficing for a pint of tea. I was contented with cold boiled bacon and bread, for I had no candles, and I could not have concentrated on the making of tea if I had. I wished to do nothing but steel my nerves to the shelling and watch the pouring rain. The gun-fire seemed eternal. Shells were shooting over the trench in one continuous stream and death lurked ever near, for in the scream of every shell was the chance of a direct hit. The limit of human misery was being reached. Men were haggard and filthy, and carried unnatural expressions. Conversation was limited and confined to short staccato sentences. Some were irritable and wished to be left alone with their emotions and their fears.

"Rum up." The very sound was inspiring.

An officer, accompanied by a sergeant, came along the trench and mess tin lids were quickly produced. Three tablespoons each, but it was sufficient to warm starved bodies and steady shattered nerves.

Certain types of people in England, warmly sheltered and well-fed, were raising their pious voices in protest at the bare idea of giving spirits to the troops. Happily, those in authority were conversant with the conditions and issued spirits as part of the winter ration. Rum was one of the greatest blessings of the war, and it never failed to renew energy and cheerfulness to otherwise tired and listless troops. Although practically a teetotaler in civilian life, I never once refused the issue in the trenches and I came to regard it as a silver lining in a black cloud of war.

A private was cursing about the weather, and the officer with the rum happened to overhear him.

"You know the little village which lies over there," he said, pointing towards the German lines.

"Grandecourt, you mean, sir," answered the man

"Yes, that's the place. Well, if it had not been for this rain, you would soon have either been occupying that place or lying somewhere in between."

Towards midday we learnt with infinite satisfaction that we were being relieved at dusk. This was two days earlier than had been expected and was wholly due to the state of the weather, for no troops can occupy water-logged trenches for any length of time and retain their efficiency. Those forty-eight hours to me had seemed as many days. Preparations were made so that when the relief came in there would be no undue delay. The contour of the ground was a great asset, for it enabled reliefs to take place during daylight. The Germans were in the low-lying ground and could not directly observe any movements beyond the front line, although, of course, their aeroplanes could spot us and get the artillery going.

At about four o'clock the first files of the relief reached us and our people began to climb over a low part of the trench on to the top.

As usual the seasoned troops, who appeared to possess a phenomenal reserve of energy, got quickly away, and it was entirely men of the new draft who began to lag behind. No amount of persuasion or abuse could make them move quicker, for the ground was treacherous and afforded no sure foothold, and at every few yards someone would fall and hold up the others I again began to feel that horrible sensation of gasping for breath which rapidly brought on an agonizing thirst. Fully half a dozen times I stumbled full length in the slimy mud, each time becoming weaker through the weight of my pack and equipment.

I became sick with exhaustion and prayed for the strength to overcome my weakness. Shells were bursting unpleasantly close, and the corporal who had been detailed to bring up the rear could be excused the curses which he flung at the poor wretches who were causing so much risk to himself.

Yard by yard we crept painfully along and at length safely reached the reserve. We had come a remarkably short distance from the supports considering how long it had taken.

Reserve quarters for two companies was an enormous earthwork known as Zollern Redoubt. Not long before, a grim struggle had been waged at this place and much evidence of it was still apparent. The unburied dead of several British regiments were still lying about, sometimes two or three in a single shell-hole where, according to the colour of the water, they had bled to death. The top of the dugout, which was almost level with the surrounding ground, was covered with irregular layers of discoloured sandbags filled with earth, and here and there was a space through which a thin wisp of smoke curled upwards to be carried away by the breeze.

The remains of a trench encircled the earthwork, and a large number of men were congregated here waiting their turn to enter.

As I came up I could hear them shouting for those down the steps to lead on, but little progress was being made. The reason was obvious. The first few men to enter found themselves in total darkness and did not proceed further than the first passage, and it was not until candles had been procured and lighted and other passages discovered that everyone was able to descend.

It was a nasty place with a musty smell, but to the troops it meant safety for the time being, and that was something. Some of the passages were wide and contained wire beds in various stages of decay. I found a nook amongst a heap of rubbish which must have been accumulating for many months. By adjusting the old tins and broken pit-props I was able to lean at a comfortable angle, using my pack for a back rest.

Directly opposite me was a passage which housed the platoon sergeant and most of his flock. More and more candles were produced and the dugout began to assume a less gloomy appearance, and with the advent of the rations and letters from home, quite a contented spirit began to prevail. By this mail I received a substantial parcel, and with the good things it contained I felt temporarily at peace with all the world.

Being in reserve was not all honey, for if a job was required to be done such as digging cable trenches, fetching ammunition, or any of the multifarious duties that can be found in trench warfare, then the men in reserve have to do it.

The only time that a man could consider himself safe for a few hours was when he had just returned from such a fatigue.

The very safety of a deep dugout conduces to nervousness, for men are reluctant to leave that safety and nothing is more awe-inspiring than to listen to the dull thud of the shells above and to realize that at any moment you are liable to be called out to undertake some risky task. As a general rule when the platoon sergeant received orders for so many men, he would take them in rotation from his roll-book, and men would listen with bated breath for their names to be called.

"Smith, Brown, Robinson, parade at the entrance immediately."

The unlucky ones would then don their kits, pick up their rifles, and creep out to see what fresh torture was in store for them.

On one such fatigue we had the task of carrying ammunition to the front line—a journey of, perhaps, three miles from the starting-point. Between them each couple of men had a box of one thousand rounds to haul. The boxes were heavy and the going hard. My companion was a big man in a big hurry to get the job done. There was a rope loop at each end of the box and my end was always so low that I got more than my legitimate share of the weight. Scrambling up and down trenches I was hopelessly at a disadvantage. The fellow cursed me violently, and I suffered agonies by the time I reached the support line.

Thereafter, the box was literally dragged along, for I had no longer the strength to lift it. With the bursting of each shell my amiable helpmate would break out into a torrent of abuse and I would abuse him in return and wish to God I had never seen a trench or a round of ammunition. I was never more thankful than when that box of ammunition had been dumped in its allotted place, and I returned to the dugout in a chastened mood.

SUPPORTS AND RESERVE

A number of times my name was called and my nerves suffered owing to the grim uncertainty of the outcome of the tasks. Ofttimes half a dozen men would set out and only three or four return, for the shelling never ceased and to walk about the top was to court death.

More than one man, who for personal reasons found it necessary to go outside, failed to return.

On the second day of our sojourn in the redoubt the word "gas" was bawled along the passages. Instantly everything was confusion. Candles were knocked over in the struggle for respirators which many had mislaid and could not find at the critical moment. Those who had cherished their gas-masks looked on from behind the safety of the goggles. Happily there was little cause for alarm. A couple of gas-shells had dropped near one of the entrances and the smouldering fragments had been speedily extinguished. Thereafter, without exception, respirators were worn at the alert.

On the fifth day orders came to prepare to move, and as rumours had been very prevalent about a march to another sector, everyone was jubilant. Early in the morning we moved away from the dreaded place, and after several hours of toiling through the mud, arrived near the village of Aveluy.

Tents were lying there in readiness to erect and the troops, working willingly, soon had a complete camp in position.

To our dismay, however, we had erected the camp for another regiment to occupy, and that same night, weary after a hard day's toil, we commenced the return journey to the redoubt.

A route was followed along the track of a light railway system. The sleepers were buried under the mud, and stepping from one to another became purely a matter of judgement. Between the sleepers and reaching far in each direction was a morass a foot or more in depth.

Cries of "steady in front" were early apparent, for the darkness was impenetrable and the track quickly became dotted with writhing men stuck in the mud.

"Keep in touch," called out the lightly-burdened officer who was taking the lead, but it was easier said than done, for we wandered helplessly on either side of the rails and became wedged, and dragged out one leg only to find that the other was as tightly held.

"I wish I could break my blarsted leg and finish with this game," cried a distressed private as he struggled and squirmed in an endeavour to extricate himself.

"Why the hell don't you go slow," came a voice from far in the rear. "I'm stuck in a perishin' hole. Go slow—will yer!"

Every now and again the leading files would halt and wait until the panting, struggling rear had formed into some kind of order and then the onward march would be resumed. The ordeal was excruciating. I felt at times that my lungs must burst with the strain imposed upon them. Hour after hour the struggle continued, and it was not until the morning was well advanced that we reached Zollern Redoubt utterly worn out in body and mind and with hearts filled with bitterness.

A few hours later we relieved the front line.

CHAPTER IV

THE FRONT LINE

HOLDING a front line is no sinecure. Alertness is demanded from each and every individual. Sentries with periscopes are posted throughout the day, and trebled during the hours of darkness. Every available man is in the trench and the dugouts are only used as company headquarters, or for specialists, such as signallers, stretcher-bearers, etc.

At all times the possibility of an enemy stunt is realized, and for safety an atmosphere of readiness must always be the premier consideration.

Regina trench had collected a couple of feet of filthy water when we took over, but fortunately we had been fitted out with gumboots, or waders, which had been brought up by a carrying party.

The pair that I obtained was many sizes too large, but they were waterproof, and I was thankful.

My first task was to scoop out a hole in the side of the trench so that I could keep my rations and cigarettes dry. I made it big enough to sit in, and had just finished and was quietly admiring it, when it started to rain again. I was glad of that hole until the water caused the top to cave in, and I had the mortification of having to dig and delve for my treasure.

This reverse either meant standing upright in the water or sitting on the sodden firestep.

Just at the point where the traverse turned was a small sap head, probably the commencement of a dugout. It was about four feet high, two of which comprised water, four feet wide, and ran barely a couple of feet into the trench. Altogether a most objectionable abode. I should never have given it a moment's thought but for one important reason—whizbangs. They began to shoot over the trench with a clearance which could have been measured in inches.

There was another man with me, and we looked at each other and then at the hole. It did not look shell-proof, but it was splinter-proof. We crawled in and tilted our "tin hats" to the front.

Man ridicules the ostrich for burying its head in the sand. There were many ostriches in the trenches during the war. Given a sheet of corrugated iron which was not even bullet-proof, and the average "Tommy" felt just about as safe as he wasn't.

We stuck that hole as long as we could and then had to come out for a rest. To say that we occupied a cramped position was putting it mildly. We could not turn, or even move, without one nearly pushing the other out, and once when a shell actually struck the side of the trench, we nearly came to blows through the commotion that it caused. We compromised by sitting down in the two feet of water.

Fortunately the shelling was spasmodic, and we were enabled to spend the greater part of the time in the trench. With the box periscope, the German trenches could be plainly seen, and it was strangely exciting to realize that in those trenches enemy troops were living, just as we were living here. Grandecourt was fully visible, and a labyrinth of trenches radiated from the village to the higher ground behind. I watched long and earnestly for some sign of life; but beyond the head of a wooden mallet which sometimes appeared above a trench where possibly repair work was in progress, the immediate view was barren of movement. No posts were held in front of the trenches in this sector, excepting a listening post which was simply the dead end of a sap driven from the main line in the direction of the enemy trenches. This post was relieved every four hours, and although I had periodical spells of duty there, nothing occurred to cause undue alarm.

During the long nights, it became the custom of many of the men to dress themselves in the overcoats which the Germans had left behind, and thus keep their own overcoats dry and consequently lighter to carry out. Sometimes enemy shrapnel helmets were worn by way of a change, and the astonishing spectacle was presented of pseudo-Germans occupying the British line.

The consumption of cigarettes among the troops was enormous, and they were the greatest nerve-restorer I ever knew. At the commencement of a strafe the first thing that a man did was to feel for his "smokes". The part that they played in the trenches has never been properly emphasized. They kept men going when the limits of endurance had been reached, and passed. A man would count his cigarettes like a miser would his gold. They were negotiable assets, tangible wealth, and the man without them was a Lazarus among his comrades. Even the army authorities recognized the value of the "smokes", for they made them part and parcel of the ordinary rations.

The stock of cigarettes required for a period in the trenches was determined beforehand, and varied according to the extent of the pocket or the capacity of the smoker. I rarely carried less than a couple of hundred for an eight-days' stretch, and these, combined with those issued, usually sufficed for all my wants.

Of course, the cadgers made inroads. It was an amazing fact that with the value set upon cigarettes in the line, certain men would invariably neglect to bring any with them, and would rely on the good nature of their comrades to keep them supplied.

Cigarettes were a boon. They may not have helped to win the war but they played a big part in making it endurable. Our stay in Regina was accompanied by many casualties. Indeed, the casualties sustained while merely holding the line were altogether out of proportion, due in the main to the tactics which the British favoured of holding the enemy trench after it had been captured. The German gunners naturally had the range of the trench to a nicety, and used their knowledge with deadly effect.

At a later date, it became the policy to dig a new line either to the front or the rear, with a heartening reduction in the casualties.

Many familiar faces of those who had left Ireland but a few weeks before were missing, and sometimes their disappearance was strikingly sudden.

Once the word was passed along the trench to tell Sergeant —— of our draft that he was wanted at company headquarters, and after a slight delay the word came back grimly and abrupt:

"Sergeant —— is dead."

The pity was that so many men were dead and buried who had been denied the pleasure of visiting their homes from the day of their enlistment.

Certain dugouts were dotted about the trench and they were big and commodious. One was fitted as a temporary hospital, and two severely wounded Germans had been left behind with food and water within easy reach. It became vitally necessary to get them away and the task, which was hazardous for the stretcher-bearers and painful to the helpless Germans, was finally accomplished. It says much for the humanity of the men upon whom the work devolved, that despite the shelling which they were compelled to endure, they carried out their task with complete regard for the comfort of the unfortunate prisoners.

The misery of wading for days on end in water which reached the knees can be better realized than imagined. Gumboots to a great extent mitigated the discomfort, but in certain parts of the trench there were holes which were not discovered until they were stepped into, and the water would then pour in over the tops of the waders. It was quite impossible to keep dry, and one's clothes always had an uncomfortable feeling of dampness about them.

Ground-sheets slipped over the shoulders were the best cover against falling rain, for they were fully waterproof, and they came to be regarded as an indispensable asset for all weathers.

By this time I was getting into a pretty hopeless state. I was caked in mud from head to foot. My clothes were heavy with water. I was weary from loss of sleep and felt thoroughly dejected. All of us were similarly placed, filthy, unshaven, and unkempt, and in appearance the officers were running us pretty close.

I was becoming vermin-ridden and accepted the position without demur.

The constant shelling was nerve-wracking, and the din of our own guns added to the strain. Approaching dusk was always heralded with increased violence on the part of the batteries and machine-guns. It always brought with it the portent of approaching disaster. The gloom which enveloped the land between disclosed terrors which daylight rendered harmless. Barbed wire stakes became advancing Germans, every shattered tree stump could become an enemy bomber. Creeping death lurked in every shell-hole.

During those fearful barrages which ravished Hessian and Regina trenches, I realized how puny and insignificant was man, whose life could be snapped like the breaking of a thread. I realized also how relatively unimportant were the common troubles which beset mankind. I looked at life in a detached kind of way, for I seemed to occupy a sphere removed from ordinary mortals who knew not war. Aims and ambitions, trials and triumphs, loves and passions, meant nothing to me. The world might still be revolving merrily for others, but my world was stopping, slowly but surely.

The tension would be relieved with a subsidence of the shelling and life would regain something of its normal appeal, but even then our outlook was limited to the present. We lived from hour to hour. We ate our food with the full knowledge that it might be the last meal we should eat, and some men invariably made a substantial meal of their rations directly they received them, and thus made sure of leaving little behind.

It was an existence both primitive and unnatural. For three days and nights we endured the discomforts of Regina, and then were relieved by the Warwicks. They had met with a hostile reception, for they had come overland in preference to the flooded trench, and it was decided that we should take the same course back.

Barely a hundred yards had been covered when a shell burst directly behind my platoon, wounding several, but fortunately not killing anyone. I felt an enormous blow in the back, but this worried me little compared with the horrible condition of the ground over which I was slipping and staggering with very little control over my feet.

Suddenly my legs shot from under me, and I literally plunged feet first into an old trench which must have contained many feet of water. I managed to dig my hands into the muddy top and hung there. When I found that I was not touching bottom and that it was quite impossible to get out unaided, I shouted for assistance, but the spirit of every man for himself and the devil take the hindermost was prevalent in those parts, and many passed with but a hurried glance in my direction.

I firmly believe that I should have drowned there and then had not one fellow with a heart of gold given me the butt of his rifle and thus enabled me to clamber out. The platoon officer then came along, and he handed me over to the care of a corporal who was bringing up the rear. The corporal was an old soldier and was as sure-footed as a mule. He soon got irritated through my inability to keep up the pace which he was making.

"We shall have a blarsted shell on top of us," he kept repeating. Want of breath hindered me from replying to his more lurid remarks.

The familiar thirst and exhaustion began to creep on me. My legs became too heavy to withdraw from the mud without strenuous labour, and I begged the corporal to go on and leave me to follow as best I could.

He cursed and raved, and with a final "Oh, go and lose yourself in the bloody German lines!" he strode away into the darkness.

I flopped down in the mud, took a long sweet drink from my water-bottle, and carefully lighted a cigarette.

I was soaked through my immersion in the water, and it was decidedly chilly, but I must have sat there a full half an hour before I decided to move. I had only the most hazy idea of my position, but keeping the Verey lights well behind and making my objective the flashing guns in the distance, I set off. Freed from the worry of having to keep up with others, I made rapid progress.

Round some shell-holes, through others, sometimes knee deep in mud, and often entangled in stray clumps of wire, and the whole of the time shells were bursting with uncomfortable regularity. At the end of an hour's struggle my objective seemed as far off as ever. It began to dawn upon me that I was lost. The Verey lights were still behind, the gun flashes still in front, but between the two, nothing but darkness and the mud underneath.

I was feeling perturbed, for to be lost in those surroundings meant that I should be obliged to wait for daylight before I could hope to locate my whereabouts. Somewhere in the direction of those guns hot soup and a good night's sleep was waiting. The very thought was inspiring, and I continued with renewed hope.

"Worcesters—this way!" sounded faintly in the distance. I could scarcely believe my own ears.

"Hallo! Where are you?" I shouted.

"Worcesters—this way!" cried the voice, and I saw the momentary flash of a lantern. I made for it and discovered that an officer with commendable foresight had established a chain of men at intervals, for the benefit of stragglers. I had missed the commencement of the chain by straying from my true course. Once on the right road the journey became easier, and I heard with a curious feeling of satisfaction that far from being the only straggler, I was but one amongst many, for at least a third of the battalion came in singly that night.

Partly to discover the position of the battalion, for no one seemed to know, and partly to find out the meaning of that sore feeling in my back, I sought a dressing-station. There I was surprised to learn that a piece of shrapnel had passed through my pack and had caused a slight wound. It was little enough, but I was ordered to report sick next day, and the outcome was that I was compelled to make journeys to an R.A.M.C. depot for inoculation.

Had I known then as much as I learnt later, I should

have made that little shrapnel puncture the basis of a pleasant sojourn down the line, for a wound, however slight to the man who knew the ropes, was an unquestioned ticket for entrance to the nearest Casualty Clearing Station. I say this unblushingly, for I never met a man who, during trench warfare, was not prepared to take a few weeks' rest from the shells and the mud whenever the opportunity was presented.

There was little hope of rejoining the battalion that night, and I had perforce to rest content on a petrol tin outside the dressing-station until morning came, and then, in the company of a great host of other stragglers, we set off for Aveluy.

CHAPTER V

BEFORE THE BATTLE

For three joyous days the Worcesters rested, and many letters were sent home and much of the canteen foodstuff consumed. The accumulation of filth was removed from clothes, and much superfluous hair from many chins. I experienced a shock when I saw my face in a mirror. Two eyes peeping through a mask of dirt and twelve days' growth of beard. I could barely recognize my own features.

The trenches of the Somme had worked havoc with my conception of soldiering. I knew now that we were slaves of war, bound securely and remorselessly to a machine which ordered systematic slaughter, that we had no hope of release, no hope for a future of comfort or security, nothing but trenches and bloodshed, day in and day out, month in and month out, until that day should come, as it must come, when the War Lords would meet and cry: "Enough!"

I realized also that the whole of Europe was a huge slave camp in a lesser degree, that our brothers and sisters, neighbours and friends, were reduced to a kind of serfdom, prostituting their skill in the manufacture of death-dealing weapons and taking pride in the production of explosives and poison gas. Was there ever such a civilization as this!

Paradoxically, the thing was absurd. Not one in a thousand, not one in ten thousand, of the men suffering the horrors of the trenches could believe in war.

Not one of the wives, or parents, or relatives of those engaged was there who would not cry from the depth of their breaking hearts, "Give us peace in our time, O God!" For the slaves of our day had learned that war was a scythe that destroys the living, creates the widow, the fatherless, the maimed, and the mad; makes heroes of one nation, devils of another, just according to which you belong. The few days I had spent in the shambles had aroused the instincts of self-preservation. I wanted no more trenches. I had seen enough of the agonies of dying men, and of the festering bodies of the dead.

The trenches were the underworld of hell!

Under those fearsome barrages men were but frightened animals, hiding from the terror. We lived in an atmosphere which was unreal. The cheery conversation sometimes carried on was but the outward and visible sign of the struggle which was raging within us, to master the emotions of fear which threatened to rise and overwhelm our manhood.

Not fear of Germans, nor of bullets, for bullets came almost silently, but fear of those awful harbingers of violent death that gave no peace, no chance. The roar of their coming, the crash of the explosion, the pungent smell, the instinctive bracing of the system, and clenching of the teeth wrought havoc with the strongest nerves.

BEFORE THE BATTLE

Men feared shell-fire more than they feared God. Those whose nerves were not strong enough to withstand the horror simply went mad in varying degrees and were admitted to hospital with shell-shock, and shell-shock was nothing less than madness born of fright. It was quite impossible to become used to shell-fire, and familiarity never could breed contempt. Rather did the continual existence under such conditions tend to reduce more and more the *morale* of the victims.

On the morning of the fourth day we moved a couple of miles nearer to the line and became engaged as working parties, which necessitated frequent journeys to the trenches. These were most uncongenial and highly dangerous, as our numerous casualties went to prove. Such things as duck-board and sheets of iron were carried up, and I can think of no more unpleasant task than the carrying of a seven-foot sheet of corrugated iron on a windy night over muddy and shell-swept ground.

Near where we were billeted lay the graves of many soldiers who had fallen at the commencement of the Somme offensive. They occupied no orderly cemetery, but were scattered haphazard over a wide area, and in one such grave, which was the object of much comment, the skull and ammunition boots of the dead man were visible. Before our departure this hasty grave was reconditioned and the tragic sight concealed for ever.

Another period was spent in Hessian and Regina trenches, and much the same procedure was gone through as before. Certain incidents are worth recording.

I was to take over a period of sentry duty at midnight and, free until that time, I decided to attempt to obtain a few hours' sleep. I had noticed a little shelter built into the side of the trench which during daytime was occupied by an artillery observer. The top was protected with sheets of iron and concealed with a covering of earth. I crept inside and was enjoying a sound sleep when a fearful crash awoke me. Amid the dust and debris I could see the stars, for a shell had blown the roof completely away, but I was quite unscathed. It was near midnight, and when I took over my duty I found that the mail had arrived and a good-sized parcel was my share. By some subtle piece of irony the Germans almost immediately placed an overwhelming barrage on the trench.

As we crouched there, knowing full well that the shelling might be the forerunner of an attack, I decided that at any rate the enemy should not have the advantage of the good things that the parcel contained, and I there and then shared it amongst the few who were with me. When the barrage was over we manned the fire-step, but no Germans came and my parcel had gone for ever.

On another occasion the captain of the company, who was a thorough sport and brave to a point of recklessness, desired a box of German bombs which he had found down a dugout in the front line, and he detailed a couple of us to accompany him. On the return journey a furious volume of shelling broke out. The trench connecting the front line and the supports was near at hand and I would gladly have availed myself of its protection, but no sign came from the officer, who walked nonchalantly ahead. The bombs were exceptionally heavy, and many times we had to change hands.

With the crashing of a salvo dangerously near, I suggested that the trench would be safer, whereupon the captain assented with a "why-did-you-not-ask-me-before" expression. Once, when the trench was being subjected to heavy fire and we were huddled against the parapet, this self-same officer walked across the top from Company Headquarters and, after coolly inquiring if everyone was all right, walked back again the way he had come.

Such behaviour when carried to the extreme is foolhardy, but undoubtedly gives the men that faith in leadership which is so essential. It is unwise to tempt Providence too far. A fortnight later this courageous officer met his death. He was fond of a stick to assist him through the mud and, upon this particular occasion while taking over the line in advance of the battalion, he was without his favourite stick and, espying a pick-handle, he climbed upon the top to secure it. A sniper immediately shot him and, although his batman managed to drag him back into the trench, he was beyond aid. His death was a great shock to the battalion, and especially to the men of his own company, who had the utmost admiration and regard for him. There were times when I had feelings akin to pity for commissioned officers of all ranks, from second-lieutenants to commanding-officer. Theirs was to give example and instil confidence. Heaven help the officer who showed fear—his authority was but a mockery. The great majority of the officers under whom I served lived up to the traditions of their rank and cast aside their personal emotions in their desire to achieve the respect of their subordinates.

. . . . .

We were again billeted at Aveluy, on this occasion in the actual ruins of the village. Cellars and first-story rooms gave ample accommodation and were infinitely more comfortable than draughty "Nissen" huts.

Another draft had arrived, and we no longer went under the designation of men of the new draft. Preparations were being made for our initiation into the mysteries of going "over the top". A battle was due to take place on the 17th of November, but for some unexplained reason it was postponed for twenty-four hours. This postponement was a personal satisfaction, for it meant another night's sleep and another day of certain life. The battalion was paraded and some details of the impending operations explained. It appeared that the objective of the brigade was Grandecourt and the immediate country to the left. Battalions of the Staffords, Warwicks, and Gloucesters were to assault, the Worcesters following with reserve supplies of bombs and ammunition. Dugouts which might contain enemy troops were to be combed out, and the advanced line then reinforced. It sounded simple enough, but how different in operation. To act as a final assistance to the troops before the attack commenced, a special tank was constructed for keeping soup hot, and was so fitted that two men could carry it in the manner of the sedan chair of olden days. Water tins were also filled with soup and a dash of rum added.

BEFORE THE BATTLE

Early on the night of the 17th, a start was made and, taking a course to the left of Aveluy, we passed through Thiepval and entered a communication trench on the right. Without event, Stuff Redoubt, a similar structure to Zollern, was reached, and the remainder of the journey commenced overland. Here began the troubles of the men who were carrying the soup. It was heavy, and only by the aid of numerous reliefs was the tank carried this far; then, as was usual, directly we entered the danger zone the pace quickened, and the soup reliefs were forgotten, with the inevitable result that the men who were carrying the tank promptly dumped it to enable them to keep up with the remainder.

On journeys of this description, when the night is dark and the route unknown, it is much more comfortable to be with the leading files, for the rear men are always straggling far behind. This is brought about by various obstructions along the route. The leading men take perhaps but a few seconds to negotiate, say, a tangle of wire, but it causes a jam, and each successive man as he clears the obstacle adds to the distance which separates front from rear. Slow though it may have seemed to the man acting as guide, it rarely failed to be anything but a rush to the tail end. Cries of "Steady in front!" were at all times a feature of any night excursion near the trenches.

After a fairly long journey we halted in trenches which seemed uncomfortably near to the German Verey lights. To me, they seemed to be well in advance of the ordinary front line, and I judged that they were enemy trenches which had been made untenable.

Star-shells were being fired in such a quantity that seemed to suggest the enemy suspected an attack was being contemplated. The officer in charge passed the word along for the soup to be brought, and seemed pained and surprised to hear that it was missing. Attention was then given to the cans, but the soup in these was frozen, and not a drop could be squeezed out. The good work of the cooks had been completely wasted. It was bitterly cold, and towards morning snow began to fall and soon the ground was covered with a white mantle which spelt ill for the hundreds of men whose khaki clothes would offer such a marked contrast to the whiteness of the snow.

The minutes dragged slowly by as we crouched in the trench talking in subdued whispers, and not daring to light a cigarette because of the close proximity of the enemy. A scuffle was heard a few yards from where I was squatting.

"Shift up a bit," came a voice.

"Keep quiet, you idiot!" whispered other voices.

"Shift up a bit, will yer; I'm sitting on a dead Jerry!"

"Christ! ain't the waiting awful," said the man nearest to me.

"Horrible," I replied. "How long does it want?"

"Zero hour's six o'clock; must be near that now. We'll know all right when they open out at the back."

I experienced a tense feeling of excitement and longed for the time to come so that we could get the job over and I could allay the anxiety that was biting into my very soul.

"Officer says it wants five minutes," I heard someone remark. Five minutes, three hundred seconds to make our peace with God. Five short minutes and the feast of the War Lords would begin—four—three—two—one——

CHAPTER VI

THE FIASCO

THE first glimmer of dawn was apparent when, with one huge convulsive roar, the barrage opened. It was like the concentrated noise and violence of a thousand thunderstorms. The sweat of mortal fear stood out on my forehead, and for a few seconds I could scarcely keep a limb still.

Almost simultaneously the frantic appeals for artillery were being fired by a distracted enemy, an appeal which was immediately answered by a volume of shells which exploded somewhere to our rear. An officer gave the signal to advance and, gripping my rifle and bayonet in one hand and a box of twelve Mills bombs in the other, I climbed out of the trench. Bullets were zipping past us, shells tearing up the ground.

The terrific din, the flashing of hundreds of bayonets, the fantastic fireworks of the Germans, presented a lurid scene. We were advancing along the slope of a ridge and in the valley on the right of us could be seen the attacking battalions for all the world like little devils rushing into hell. Behind them came the Engineers, paying out cable and working hastily amid the inferno that was raging. Officers were dressed as privates and were indistinguishable among the general mass of rank and file. On the back of every man was a great yellow patch which showed conspicuously—it was the guide for Air Force observers, and a target for German riflemen should a man get wounded and attempt to return in daylight.

I had covered some two hundred yards when I was detailed by an officer to bomb a dugout.

"Clear them out!" he declared abruptly, and then, noting that there were several entrances, he promptly detailed another man to assist.

Without more ado I produced a bomb and, withdrawing the pin, sent it down the first entrance. It exploded with a satisfying crash, and a similar method was adopted for each opening. There being no response I dispatched a smoke bomb on the same errand.

Nothing happened, and so we were able to conclude that either the dugout was empty or that its occupants had been killed. I did not mind which so long as personal safety was assured.

The light was increasing, and I was in something of a quandary, for the companies had gone beyond our vision. I was quite uncertain as to the ultimate direction they had taken, but by now they must certainly have reached their objective. We mutually agreed that the best thing we could do was to lie there until visibility was better and then try to reach them after we had got our bearings. Good cover was difficult to find, for we were on the side of a steep ridge nearest to the German line and some cover was vitally necessary. Eventually we found a small shell-hole and, placing our boxes of bombs out of rifle-fire, we lay there. Presently renewed firing broke out, and peering cautiously over the edge of the shell-hole we were astounded to see a German trench some eighty yards away thickly manned by the enemy who, fully exposed, were firing at anything which moved. Where, then, was our battalion and the remainder of the brigade? It seemed inexplicable. It would have been a simple matter to have picked off several Germans, for they offered admirable targets, but that would have necessitated giving away our own position with ultimately certain death.

To the army I was but a number, a grain of sand in a mighty desert, a private at a shilling a day, but I was also an individual with but one life, and I did not intend to jeopardize that life by thoughtless indiscretion or misguided enthusiasm.

Bullets were now flying thickly above us, and we judged that the enemy was firing at living targets, most probably men who were lying out in exposed positions, or wounded who were attempting to crawl to safety. One such man with a bullet through his foot did manage to drag himself into the shell-hole, and from him we heard that the attacking waves had met with overwhelming opposition, that some British had occupied enemy trenches and others driven back. He himself had been shot down before the objective was reached and had crawled from shell-hole to shell-hole. He stayed but a few minutes and then continued on his perilous journey, and I never saw him again.

Towards nine o'clock the snow turned to rain, and

for the remainder of the day it poured incessantly, soaking us to the skin and partly filling the shell-hole.

No movement was now possible without involving the greatest risk, for the enemy had settled down to occasional sniping, and even a loose board swinging on the side of a dugout not many yards away was constantly being riddled with bullets.

My comrade in distress belonged to the newest draft and it was his first time in. He was a heavily-built man, perhaps forty years of age, and was emphatically cool. I believe that he had the impression, like I myself had in Hessian trench, that this kind of adventure was the usual thing to be expected. His optimism was refreshing, and he seemed quite confident that he would survive the perils of the trenches and return to his home in due course. Mention of his family brought a shade of pathos into the tone of his voice.

"Only a fortnight ago, mate, I was home with the wife and kids," he said. "Four bonny youngsters I've got. They think I'm on a sort of a trip, and I've promised to take 'em some rock back, but the missus, she knows better; she left me with a smile, but I'll bet the pillow's wet with tears every night."

"How the deuce did you come to enlist?" I asked, thinking of the heavy responsibilities which he possessed.

"The Derby scheme," he replied. "Mind you, I didn't think they'd call on me so quick, but I'm here, and here I've got to stay for the duration. Rotten hole, mate, isn't it?"

"About the worst we shall get, I hope," was my reply.

"How long have we got to stick this? Don't seem any earthly use in hanging about here any longer than we can help. I suppose we shall have to wait till we're relieved, anyhow," he said.

"We don't stay here after dusk," I answered. "We're not holding the line; the fact of the matter is, I don't know where the line is, and we're not going to potter about this district looking for a place that might not exist. We're looking for a safer place where there's a chance of getting some grub and a sleep. Another thing, there's a trench filled with Jerrys over there that I can't make top nor tail of. According to my reasoning, that trench ought to be our support or reserve line if the attack had been successful."

"Well, what's happened?" said my companion.

"Haven't the faintest idea," I replied, "unless the blighters in that trench laid low until our chaps had crossed over."

"If that's it, the sooner we get out the better," said he.

We mutually agreed that immediately it became dark we would strike back to our rear lines. The right direction we expected to find easily, but it would necessitate the utmost caution because of the nearness of the Germans. Slowly the hours passed, and the rain and the cold numbed our limbs so that we rubbed them vigorously to restore the circulation. There was nothing to break the monotony of the vigil. We lay on our backs with our heads pointing to the German line. Our immediate view was the crest of the ridge along which we had advanced, and the dugout which we had fruitlessly bombed lay a little to the left. Looking in each direction we could see nothing but the slope of the ridge, clumps of broken wire, and hummocky ground. We dared not smoke, but happily we had the day's rations in our haversacks, and we were enabled to enjoy a satisfactory meal swilled down with a drink from our water-bottles. I had a tin of pork-and-beans, some meat, and a fairly big chunk of bread, and my companion was the happy possessor of a tin of cooked vegetables, half of which should have been shared with another man who, by the look of things, had precious little chance of getting it.

For one blessing I was devoutly thankful—our cumbersome packs had been left behind at the transport lines and we were equipped in so-called fighting-order, the haversack being strapped on the back. This reduced the weight considerably, and was a distinct advantage when muddy ground had to be negotiated.

Twilight began to deepen, and rifle and machine-gun fire was renewed with vigour. Calmly we prepared to make our departure. The bombs we decided to leave behind, for the less impedimenta the quicker we might get away. It became dark enough to peer over the edge of the shell-hole with safety. The German trench had disappeared in the gloom. We stood up and stretched our legs and then made rapidly for the trench that we had started from.

In two minutes we were lost. The ground was unrecognizable and the several objects I had in mind were not visible. I remembered seeing a couple of dead Germans lying side by side and also a heap of broken trench-boards, but the lay of the land seemed to have altered. We found several trenches, but none of them corresponded with the one which we were seeking, and all of them were more or less filled with mud and water.

The darkness became a menace and we were in mortal danger of straying into the German front line. Mud channels and bits of trenches ran in all directions. A star-shell would soar into the air, flooding the ground with light and, standing quite still, we would try to locate our position, but there was nothing which would serve as a guide, and the light would fade away leaving us completely bewildered.

How long we wandered I cannot say, but suddenly I saw a tiny glow. It was the lighted end of a cigarette, and I knew that behind that cigarette was a human being. But who? German or British? We quietly debated the point, and then decided to risk a closer inspection. Now and again, the glowing end would disappear and we would wait until it showed again. Cautiously we crept towards it. There was a decided danger of getting shot by whoever they were, for creeping figures are not tolerated in front of the trenches. We began to hear voices, but could not distinguish the tongue.

"They're perishin' Jerrys!" whispered my companion.

Then a sharp challenge rang out, and the words were music in our ears.

"Stop where you are!" And then: "Who the hell are you?"

"Worcesters," we cried, simultaneously. "'D' Company."

Satisfied with our identity they invited us into the trench, and we discovered with a certain amount of satisfaction that we had fallen in with the battalion Lewis gun section. Barely had we become settled when a fierce British barrage opened. We immediately thought that a German counter-attack had been launched and some confusion was apparent, heightened by the fact that the gunners had very little ammunition, having lost the major part of it coming in when the mule which was carrying it fell into a deep shell-hole filled with water. We endured hell listening to that barrage and knowing nothing of what was taking place, and it would be appropriate to explain here what actually occurred.

Sir Arthur Conan Doyle in his "British Campaign in France and Flanders, 1916", describing the battle of the Ancre, says that while the Gloucesters were successful in seizing the west end of Grandecourt, the other three battalions—Warwicks, Worcesters, and North-Staffs—fared ill, owing to numerical weakness, lack of knowledge of the ground, loss of direction, bad weather, and deadly machine-gun fire. He states that the garrison of the German trenches appeared to have been as numerous as the storming British and far more advantageously placed. "Half of the North-Staffords reached their objective but were isolated, and either killed or taken prisoners; and an attempt on part of the Cheshires to get in touch with their lost comrades later in the evening only served to swell the casualty lists."

Quite unaware that the Cheshires were attacking, we stood in that trench ready to attempt to repel any assault which might be made, but after a time the shelling ceased and a certain quietness reigned.

The Lewis gunners informed us that they were expecting to be relieved at any moment and suggested that we should wait and return with them, for, as one put it, "You won't find your way out without a guide; you'll walk round and round and get no further and perhaps find yourselves in Jerry's lines before you've finished."

So we waited through the long night, but no relief came, and towards dawn I was so thoroughly hungry and miserable I suggested that we should make an attempt to get away. My companion agreed immediately. He was quite prepared to follow me, for I was a veteran with my month of trench warfare compared with his thirty-six hours.

The trench ran partly up the ridge, but there was an open space, which had been ploughed up by constant shelling, that would have to be crossed before the safety of the reverse slope could be reached. We decided that just before dawn would be the best time to get away, for it would enable us to cross the ridge and shelter on the other side until it was light enough to see the route.

Unfortunately, just as we were on the point of making our departure, an enemy protective barrage was launched which was so intense that we were glad to seek safety in a lower part of the trench. This strafe lasted until it was fully light, but did not deter our resolve to get away. We crept on hands and knees to the very end of the trench on the ridge and there paused for the final rush. Barely five yards was all that was necessary to cover. We darted out together, ran low, and flung ourselves on the other side. Three rifle shots rang out, and we heard the bullets zip perilously near, but we were out of that accursed valley and nothing more mattered for the moment.

Looking round, I could not see anything which was familiar or which was likely to assist us back to the rear lines. The broken shell-battered ground stretched far away to the left, to the right, and to the front. Here and there a few tree-stumps, and in the distance a disabled tank, which apparently was on fire, for smoke was issuing from it and muffled reports suggested that the ammunition it contained was exploding.

Many corpses, both British and German, were lying about—some with blackened faces and shattered limbs. Others in the process of decomposition had disclosed the teeth to such an extent that they were already embryo skeletons. Not two yards away lay the buttocks and legs of what was once a man—a Britisher! Somebody's husband, somebody's son. Perhaps even now a distant family was waiting with aching heart for the letter which could never come, and those buttocks and legs would lie there day after day until such time when the spectre of death had moved further afield and the place was safer and a fatigue-party with shovels would dig a rude grave, asking themselves how many more had they got to bury before they could get away. I found myself wondering what sort of a man he was, where was the other half, and would he get two burials?

I was aroused from my reverie by my companion, who suggested making a move as we were in the place where the shells dropped pretty frequently.

We took no needless risks, and literally crawled until we reached a trench which appeared to be running in the direction that we wished to go. The trench was deep in mud and water and so we kept to the top. Several hundred yards away came a khaki-clad figure ploughing through the mud. I was about to hail him when we heard the ping of a rifle bullet and the man dropped like a stone. The bullet had apparently come from nowhere, but taking the broad hint we jumped into the trench and waded through it. The trench led us to the position where the man had fallen, and we found him with his head not two feet from the edge. He was quite dead, and a red patch on his leather jerkin showed where the bullet had struck. Who he was, what brought him there, and where he was bound for we should never know. It seemed so infernally mysterious. So far as I was able to make out the German line should be out of observation, but it was quite evident that this particular spot was marked.

We began to find evidence to prove that the trench was the right one. A broad white tape trailing as far as the eye could see was proof positive, and I sighed with relief. A dugout in the trench attracted our attention. I had often thought of collecting a few souvenirs which would be of interest at some future happy date. We decided to attempt a little exploration, and we gingerly descended the muddy steps until we reached the bottom, from where a single passage ran in one direction.

I struck a match and was horrified by a ghastly spectacle. It was a shambles. Dead men, Germans, covered the floor of that passage, some lying, others stooping over them, and one propped up with his back to the wall, leering at the entrance as if he had expected some such visit. We retreated up the steps with indecent haste. How they could have died like that was something of a problem, for the throwing of bombs down the entrance would not accomplish so much. Possibly gas-shells had accounted for the tragedy.

After covering a considerable distance we calculated that it would be perfectly safe to follow the tape overland. We knew that the tape was a sure guide, for it was laid for that very purpose.

A couple of Tommies lying by the side with full kits reminded us that we had been warned to make up any deficiency before we returned to billets and, as my ground-sheet had become detached and lost, I had the unpleasant duty of commandeering one that belonged to the dead. Our rifles were pitiful objects. They were rusty and so caked with mud that only a thorough washing and careful oiling would induce them to fire again.

A man clings to his rifle in the trenches for obvious reasons, and whatever else he may dump when exhausted his rifle will always be safely in his possession. The greatest disgrace one could incur, other than sheer cowardice, was to return from the line without arms, and I have known a man who had the misfortune to lose his, coolly return with a piece he had picked up and, explaining that it had been hit by a shell, had it exchanged for another. That was the beauty of the system. Produce the remnant of an article and it could readily be exchanged for something whole, but woebetide the man who had lost part of his kit and had nothing but excuses to exchange. He would have the company quarter-master fuming and grousing, and get threatened with all sorts of stoppages from his pay.

We found what was left of "D" Company in the trench which led to Thiepval. They had just breakfasted and cleaned up all the rations between them.

"Thought you were dead," said a sergeant. "You'll have to make shift with a couple of biscuits till we reach billets. They didn't send up much in the way of rations."

"Where are the others?" I queried, for I could not see more than thirty at the most.

"Over there where you've just come from," he replied. "Haven't you seen any more knocking about?"

I told him of what had occurred, and asked him how they had got away. He said that he hardly knew. They had just crept back in ones and twos and collected at this point.

I chewed my biscuits reflectively. The company had started well over a hundred strong and a mere handful had returned. Of course, a percentage would have gone to the Casualty Clearing Stations, but it was equally certain that scores of dead and dying were still over there. I began to scrutinize those who had come back, and I was shocked to find that several valued friends were missing. The platoon officer had not been seen from the moment the attack started, and he was never again heard of.

We stayed in the trench for the greater part of the day, and two more weary men returned from the dreaded wastes beyond, and towards evening we marched back into Aveluy, back to the very same billets we had left but a short time before.

But how different! Once so crowded with chattering troops, and now too much room, too little chatter.

I listened to the roll-call. You could have heard a pin drop as the sergeant-major began his task.

Name after name was called in vain.

In some instances a man was known to have been killed or wounded and eye-witnesses vouched for it, but with the majority they simply did not answer.

The next day we were ready to march away. Rations had been issued and, as a full company had been catered for, every man had double his share and much still remained. There was a hard and fast rule that billets must be handed over to the incoming unit clean and free from refuse and lumber, and this evidently included surplus rations, for I was detailed with several others to bury half a cheese, several loaves of bread, and innumerable tins of jam, bully, and cigarettes.

It was a fearful waste, but it was military etiquette, and that is about all that can be said of it. We paraded in the derelict street of Aveluy. The band took up its position at the head of the skeleton battalion. The commanding officer on his horse gave the order to march, and we swung along the road that led to safety.

Far in the rear in that fearful valley facing Grandecourt the bodies of our comrades were lying, seeing nothing, hearing nothing, and the drums and fifes were churning out: "Keep the home fires burning, While your hearts are yearning", and at home a methodical War Office was compiling names and numbers for dispatch to the wives or parents of the men who had passed on to the greater valley beyond.

CHAPTER VII

HÉBUTERNE

THE Worcesters spent Christmas in a little village of the name of Gezincourt, only a short distance from the town of Doullens. It was a dilatory place, with an uninteresting population. Its streets were mean and dirty, and its shops few and sparsely stocked. The villagers seemed poor and dressed badly, but on Sunday mornings they put away their workaday attire and for two hours revelled in their gayest raiment and early morning Mass.

Some houses specialized in supplying the inner man which the army rations had failed to satisfy, and they made many francs by so doing. The estaminets sold weak beer and did likewise.

Very pleasant had been those few weeks removed from the horrors of the trenches, although much hard work had been accomplished in the way of training, for a battalion out of the line can find as much to do in a week of rest as an average citizen would find in a week of hard work. The shining of buttons and buckles, and the scrubbing of packs and equipment, was becoming a fetish. "Soldiers' Friend" in penny tins and khaki "Blanco" in twopenny slabs was bought as eagerly as in the canteens during training at home. Dirty buttons meant a crime, and a crime meant pack-drill, and pack-drill was harsh and uncomfortable.

Soon after our arrival a bathing parade was arranged. It was the first bath I had had for ten weeks, and I badly wanted it, and it was the longest time I was forced to wear the same underlinen without a change. From then onwards the facilities in this respect definitely improved, and it was a rare occurrence to wait longer than three or four weeks without a visit to the baths. They were nearly always shower baths, and it was a cold operation during the winter months, for the establishment was often a temporary affair with wet floors and a keen wind blowing through innumerable cracks. We would undress in a draughty outer room and stand shivering under the sprays a dozen at a time. A couple of minutes would be allowed for the soap to be rubbed in, and then a couple of minutes while it was swilled off, and the water would be turned off in readiness for the next batch. A change of underlinen, which had belonged to some other unit and had undergone a stoving process, would then be issued, and the bathing parade was over.

I had voluntarily joined the Lewis gun section, and had spent much time and study in learning the details of this useful little weapon of destruction. It was not a popular hobby by any means, and many fought shy of being connected with the gunners, but I was attracted to it because they apparently led a freer existence. I abhorred the parades and routine of company work, and I never regretted the day when I cast in my lot with the Lewis gunners. It was not that I was becoming reconciled to war, or that I thought I could kill Germans quicker with a Lewis, but I was reconciled to the solid fact that I had got to make the best of a bad job. At the present time the personnel of the sixteen guns paraded and billeted together, but at a later date they were split up into the ratio of four to a company. The privileges of the gunners were, however, maintained during the remainder of my time in France.

As a general rule, eight men comprised a gun-team—Number One had sole charge of the gun, Number Two the bag of spare parts, the remainder being ammunition carriers. Of course, each man was taught the mechanism and had ample range instruction, for shells do not discriminate. A man might go into the trenches as a Number Four, and return the proud possessor of the gun.

At Gezincourt I became acquainted with "Shorty", a man well over six feet in height, with great broad shoulders and the courage of two ordinary men. He was anything but handsome, would have made a good nigger with his face blackened, liked the nickname of Shorty, and had a disposition which was singularly amiable. A favourite with officers and men alike, Shorty became to me a faithful and staunch pal, whom, as I like to put it, would gladly fetch you in if ever you were lying out near the wire.

Shorty was my instructor on the gun, and so proficient was he that when he had finished I knew the Lewis from A to Z. I did not immediately become attached to the team of which he was the leader; that came at a later date, but I saw much of him, and our friendship ripened with the passing of time.

Whatever he was in civilian life I was never quite sure. Shorty was a conundrum that had never been effectively solved. He was very secretive about his past and invariably declared that he was a burglar by profession, but I rather think that by his knowledge and love of flowers he betrayed himself as a gardener.

Another fellow with whom I became intimate was Mark Lane, a rather effeminate kind of a chap with a handsome face and a fairly strong nerve; and between these two I rapidly developed those soldierly qualities of "sticking it", which I had so much lacked on the muddy wastes of the Somme.

The billets of the gunners was a large house taken over by the military. In each room wire beds had been erected in tiers, and I occupied a berth nearest the ceiling. Ground-sheets were spread over the wire-netting, but the men underneath were in a constant state of irritability because of the crumbs and odds and ends which, despite precaution, would persist in falling through sundry exposed places. Naturally, it was most annoying for a man to find half a candle in his can of tea, or a blob of jam on his tunic; but then they had other advantages, such as getting out on parade while we were being cursed for taking so long over it. With all its shortcomings, it was a hotel compared with some billets I had lived in.

At the back of the house was a brook, and every morning the banks were thronged with troops washing hands and faces and sometimes chests, and shaving with the aid of mirrors stuck on convenient trees. Shaving was usually a painful process, for the razor was ever blunt and the water icily cold, and neither was sufficient excuse for appearing unshaven on parade. How I envied those whose downy deposit could never by any stretch of imagination be construed into the definition of beard.

Early in January the battalion, strengthened by the inclusion of a large draft, marched away from these congenial quarters, and two days later we entered the village of Hèbuterne.

This village could almost be said to be in the trenches; in fact, the communication trenches led directly from it. Hèbuterne must have been distinctly superior to many of the villages of the Somme. There were more streets and better-class houses, although they were in a sorry condition through much shelling. We quickly found the danger of loitering in the streets, and at one point, the cross-roads, it was suicidal to linger, for machine-gun fire raked it with devilish accuracy. The water supply was confined to wells, and water fatigue was an unpleasant job, for more often than not just as a pail of water was being nicely hauled to the top a couple of shells would explode within smelling distance, and he was a very cool man who did not let go the windlass and seek temporary shelter.

Our gun-team had been attached to Headquarters and was withheld from the trenches for any emergency which might arise. We hoped nothing would happen, for we had discovered a nice little billet with one room quite intact, but after the first day we began to think quite seriously that we should be far better off in the line.

Casualties in the front line necessitated a couple of graves being dug, and we had orders to dig them in the little cemetery on the outskirts of the village. It was a horrible task, this digging of graves for one-time pals. It filled one with an emotion which was inexpressible. Six feet long, six feet deep, and three wide was the instruction, and when they were completed we went to the improvised mortuary for the bodies. They were wrapped in a mummified fashion with strips of sandbagging through which the blood had oozed and discoloured. A stretcher on wheels was provided, and the cortège commenced to wend its way through the village streets. A shell came whistling over and burst with an ear-splitting crash in a part which we must pass. Then came another which took away part of a roof. A salvo screamed overhead, and the pace quickened into a trot, and then a run, and finally into a headlong gallop.

Down the long street we raced, with the stretcher jolting unceremoniously, not daring to pause until we reached the cemetery. Close to the far side of the graveyard lay a battery and, in endeavouring to put the guns out of action, the enemy had made sad havoc of many of the graves which held the remains of the departed of Hèbuterne. As we reached the two newly-dug graves it was quite evident that the battery was enduring a severe strafe, for black shrapnel was bursting in the air and high explosives throwing up columns of earth and spraying fragments of iron in every direction.

Complete reverence under such conditions was impossible, not even with a Chaplain, and the service was distinctly hurried. Steel hats in hand and hearts beating violently, we followed each word with controlled impatience. The sonorous voice of the Padre, the silent figures, the scream of the shells, and then a grave that was too short. Frantically we dug away more earth, and still the shells burst, and the blood mounted to our foreheads, and we knew that more graves would be necessary if we did not hurry. The last rites were observed, the earth thrown in with indecent haste, and we cleared out of that grim cemetery without further delay.

Back in the billet we lit a fire, for dusk was approaching, but the wood was damp and would not burn, and an ingenious youth pushed in a couple of Verey lights to help it along. It blazed! I have never seen a fire blaze better. It would have fired the remains of the house, but it was kicked outside and must have caused a glare in the sky for the German gunners planted several shells in the vicinity, and we left the fire to look after itself while we sought safety in an evil-smelling cellar.

Later, when it became quiet, we crept back and made a better job of the fire, but it smoked abominably, nevertheless, and my eyes smarted and ached until I was forced to make periodical visits into the fresh air to secure relief.

Cards were produced, and a game of "brag" commenced, and it developed from halfpennies to pounds and pounds, which the players did not possess and had no hope of ever possessing, so that when far into the night the game was finished and the losses totalled some hundreds, the winner would gladly have accepted twopence and called the matter square. We slept, or, rather, dozed, round the brazier for the remainder of the night, and I woke up once with a peculiar sensation in my left leg and was just in time to prevent my puttee from being quite burnt through.

The whole of the next day we were engaged in sandbagging the dugouts of battalion headquarters, rather heavy work and decidedly dusty, and taking all these incidents into consideration I was not altogether upset when a runner brought us orders to proceed immediately to an outpost. We followed a guide to a point two or three hundred yards in front of the first line trench, and settled down in a sap-head which was chiefly furnished with empty bully-beef tins. The gun was mounted in a convenient position which offered a wide expanse of fairly level ground, and magazines of ammunition were placed near, the whole being covered with a ground-sheet to protect them from the damp and possible rain.

The holding of a post was a revelation to me, and yet I found it distinctly agreeable. It gave one a sense of responsibility and an opportunity to use the brains and the eye and, what was better, a freedom from the irksome duties of the trenches. Its perfect solitude, its uncanny stillness, its atmosphere of imminent peril, sometimes subconscious, sometimes apparent, kept one in a constant state of alertness.

During the hours of daylight the occupants of a post are completely isolated and assistance cannot be procured under any circumstances. If the enemy makes a raid, the post must hold its own or be blotted out of existence, and if a man is wounded he must lie there until he can be got away under cover of darkness. The one solid advantage of an outpost was its comparative immunity to shell-fire, for if the Germans held a similar post, which they usually did, their artillery was bound to exercise due caution for fear of shelling their own men. Sometimes during the night an enemy shell would burst between the opposing posts, and without fail the Germans would fire a rocket with its cascade of golden rain, a signal to the batteries that shells were dropping short, and the ensuing rounds would pass comfortably over both posts and burst well to the rear. My companions, among whom was Mark Lane, were fully seasoned to the work of holding posts. Their coolness was refreshing, due perhaps to a large extent to the absence of excessive shelling. They chatted and dozed, argued and joked, and contrived generally to impart some life to an otherwise tame procedure.

I was the only one who possessed a watch, and it was found distinctly useful as a medium for relieving sentries. We did spells of one hour each, and it was a mystery to me why day dawned at such an unearthly hour, and when night fell at two p.m. I realized that the lending of the watch to each successive sentry was no good for the watch, for evidently the fingers had been pushed round to shorten the spell of duty. Argument was of no avail, for it was pointed out to me that a cook who had previously borrowed the watch had prepared breakfast at 8 a.m. instead of 7 a.m., and received a severe reprimand in consequence. Little of note happened, and in the evening we were brought back to the front line, which was fairly deep in water. From this part of the line many men were sent away suffering from that painful malady—trench-feet. This was occasioned by exposure to cold and water, and even gumboots were not always sufficient to ward off its attacks. Whale-oil was issued as a preventive, and this had to be rubbed into the feet every morning, an operation which was usually watched by an N.C.O., for the men would rarely submit to it without coercion.

It required a certain amount of agility to perform, for the leg would have to be held out of the water, trench-boot and sock removed, and the oil applied while the man balanced himself as best he could.

Whether the whale-oil was beneficial I could not say, but our superiors evidently thought so, for the system was strictly adhered to. From the point of view of the shirker, or the "had enoughs", or by whatever word or phrase those who were sick of war could be best described, trench-feet was a boon, a sail appearing over a murky horizon. It sent men hobbling but smiling along the route which led to sleep and comfort and safety. They went by the dozen, and regardless of heroics or patriotism they were glad they were going. Some men seemed immune from the disease, and to my own knowledge one fellow stood in icy water for ten consecutive hours without moving and at the end of that time his feet were as healthy as before. He was deeply disappointed, for he had hopefully anticipated a few weeks' rest at the base.

Our stay at Hèbuterne lasted about eight days, after which we were again on the march. I was not pleased, for there were many worse places. The trenches were more accessible than those I had previously experienced. We had been able to enjoy hot soup in the line and, although strafes had taken place, they had never reached the pitch of the nerve-shattering barrages of Regina.

CHAPTER VIII

A "STUNT"

THE country was frostbound and the roads which, until recently, had been almost impassable, were dry and pleasant to walk upon. The cold was intense, and the inhabitants of Bertrancourt, whose water-supply had long since frozen, were glad to take advantage of the elaborate pumping installation erected by the Engineers for army needs.

The Worcesters were billeted in huts leading away from the main street of the village, the Lewis gun section occupying quarters a mile removed from the companies. Three gun-teams were allotted to a hut, and I found that Shorty, with his crew, were to be our temporary bed-fellows. Across the road was a negro camp, and the poor fellows, unaccustomed to such rigorous climate, were habitually walking about draped in army blankets. They were inveterate cadgers, and to produce a cigarette-case within view of any of them was the signal for an immediate rush and clamorous cries of "Cigarette, Tommy!" It was quite a common occurrence for the huts to be invaded by negroes on a similar quest, and from objects of curiosity they developed into an infernal nuisance.

A "STUNT"

Owing to the scarcity of water, washing became a luxury, and one canvas pail usually had to suffice for all the men who cared to use it. Of course, no one would openly declare that he did not want to wash, but the very thought of divesting one's clothing with a freezing wind blowing was in itself a deterrent. Shorty always made extensive preparations for his ablutions. He would heroically divest himself of his tunic, strop his razor, produce a microscopic piece of soap and a towel, and approach the bucket like an all-the-year-round swimmer. Then his face would undergo a change, and his eyes would flash.

"Who the hell's been in here?" he would yell, knowing full well that perhaps half a dozen had already used the water. "Look at the scum. Can't wash myself in that," and with a sigh he would return to his kit, produce his water-bottle, and scour his face and neck with a shaving-brush. The hut possessed a stove and, in the absence of other fuel, it became the practice to search the surrounding district for wood, and woebetide the man who did not contribute his share. His rights to a warm were immediately questioned, and until he repaired the deficiency by producing something which would burn he was an Ishmael among his fellows. That stove worked overtime during our occupation of the huts, and if it could have talked it would have supplied the answer to the mystery which surrounded the disappearance of many duck-boards from a nearby dump.

Soldiers pass their spare time in divers ways. Some settle down immediately after parade and write voluminous letters, and seem to enjoy doing so; others give their buttons and boots an extra brush and seek the comforts of the nearest estaminet, where until eight o'clock a sing-song could always be indulged in. Schools of gamblers could be found in every hut or tent, and brag, pontoon, and bank flourished exceedingly.

Certain men favoured getting the bed, or "kip", down directly it was dark and, with a candle stuck on a jam tin, they would read contentedly until the warning notes of "Lights Out" brought the day officially to a close.

One boisterous night was spent, that was when arrears of rum were brought up to date and each man had five days' issue to come. We formed a queue and received the arrears in instalments of three tablespoons each, and when the current date was reached not a man was there but who was not smiling very broadly indeed. An impromptu concert was arranged and might have been hugely successful, but everyone wanted to sing at once, and the result brought the negro campers over *en masse*. When they had been got rid of half of the budding artistes were asleep and the other half nodding, and a few minutes later, the sergeant who paid his nightly visit to ascertain if all were present was greeted with such a sustained volume of snoring that for once he was obliged to make a guess.

We knew that those billets were too comfortable to last long, and we were right, for on the fourth day the battalion was passing through Colincamps on the road to the trenches.

Two or three kilometres from Colincamps was

Euston dump, where Engineers and trench equipment was stored, and from near this point the communication trench ran to the support line. It was an easy journey with comparatively little shelling, and the ground being hard with frost the going was sure.

This sector had once belonged to the enemy and, as usual, was fitted extensively with the spacious dugouts which we found so convenient. It must have been a bitter pill for the Germans to realize that the fruits of their years of labour lay in our hands, and they were ever-ready to do their utmost to smash in the entrances and so make them untenable. For us, of course, the dugouts were always on the wrong side of the trench and were liable to receive a direct hit. Gas-shells were a particular bane, and on the outside of some dugouts brass shell-cases were swinging with a sentry always on duty, whose orders were to strike the gong immediately gas was suspected.

The trenches abounded in rats of a huge size, and it was a common sight to see them running about the top in search of food. As before, our gun-team was attached to Headquarters, and we were allotted a dugout somewhat smaller than the average. There we passed four uneventful days and nights, sitting or lying around a coke and charcoal fire, bleary-eyed and half-stupefied with the fumes, counting the hours to when we should be relieved, and hoping against hope that we should be allowed to lie in the stinking atmosphere undisturbed until that time.

It was during our second spell in these trenches that things began to happen. A raid was planned for the Sunday night, and some snow having fallen, white smocks were provided for the raiding party.

Shorty was picked to go over, and the team to which I belonged was divided into two parts. We were to occupy a small sap called Robin Post, well in advance of the front line, and our particular task was to cover the returning raiders and, if found necessary, attempt to repulse the enemy counter-raid should one be organized. It was arranged that half of the gun-team should hold Robin Post from just before the commencement of the stunt until five o'clock in the morning, at which time they would be relieved by the other half. The spin of a coin was the deciding factor, and I found that I was to accompany the five o'clock party.

Towards the time fixed for the raid the snow was insufficient to hide the colour of the ground, but the original scheme was adhered to, and the men went over offering better targets than was intended.

Mark and I, with the two other men, adjourned to the dugout, for when the barrage opened it would be exceedingly unwise to remain in the trench. Soon we began to hear the monotonous thud of enemy shells and felt the vibration of direct hits on the earth above. Time and again the candles were extinguished by the sudden rush of air which followed the explosions. I was very thankful that we had been vouchsafed such a haven of refuge.

Towards one o'clock in the morning we were sitting near the fire smoking and wondering how the raid was progressing when we were startled by the sudden appearance of the Lewis gun officer.

He was pale and agitated.

"Come on, you fellows!" he said quietly. "The post has been wiped out!"

We strapped on our equipment and followed him up the dugout steps. Huge shells were crashing near the trench. The fierce rattle of machine-gun fire was proceeding all along the line, for the Germans were alarmed and annoyed. We passed from the supports along the communication trench and, midway to the front line, the officer climbed out of the trench and led the way over the exposed ground. It was distinctly unnerving, for high explosives were tearing up the ground around us, and several times we threw ourselves on the earth and heard the razor-like pieces of iron whizzing above.

The section of the front line over which we passed was choked with wounded whose white smocks were daubed with crimson patches. Men of the R.A.M.C. were attending them under conditions of the gravest danger.

At last, Robin Post! Two of our men were lying dead, a third severely wounded and partially blind. The remaining member of the half-team had dashed for the rear lines, demented and raving.

Mark and I bent over one of the dead men who had been a particular friend. A piece of shrapnel had pierced his steel helmet and, passing through his skull, had come out under his chin. We were shocked to discover that a finger of his right hand was missing; more so when we remembered that the finger had once held a ring. His wristlet-watch, too, had disappeared. Some fiendish ghoul had been at work. In justice to the millions of good soldiers, I hasten to add that this revolting incident was unique, and never again did I see or hear of anything appertaining to the despoiling of the dead.

Robin Post was a sap which had been burrowed into a ridge for about five yards. There were many of these saps scattered about, commenced probably with the intention of using them for mining operations and abandoned for various reasons. The ridge offered ample protection from shells which burst to the front, but directly behind there was nothing to stay the flying fragments which followed every explosion.

A couple of wounded men lay on stretchers in the sap, one of them being a corporal with whom I had been associated in Ireland. His leg was shattered, and as he was about to be carried away I shook him warmly by the hand and wished him the best of luck, and he smiled contentedly and wished me luck also, and a more cheerful soul could not have been found in those trenches on that night. Months later, I was delighted to hear that he was going on well and, although reduced to the wearing of an artificial limb, was happy in his return to civilian life.

The heavy shelling was sustained throughout the remainder of the night, but stretcher-bearers continued to search the ground for wounded who might still be lying out. The groans and cries which we had first heard coming from various directions ceased as the work progressed, and with the dawn the last sign of the raid had disappeared.

The knowledge that we were occupying a proved death-trap was not inspiring, and our conversation and demeanour was anything but cheerful. We clung to the side of the ridge and hoped for the best, and when daylight came and we were alone we settled down in the sap to await the return of dusk.

I heard many stories of Shorty and that raid, of how he crossed the German front line with only one comrade and caught some of the enemy in flight, and of how he worked like a Trojan bringing in wounded, but as these reminiscences are authentic I mention this with due reserve. The advantage gained by the raid was nil. We occupied no new trenches; we had not taken a prisoner. We had certainly given the enemy a fright, and we had paid the price in dead, wounded, and missing. What happened to the Worcesters was happening nightly to many regiments, and was rarely of sufficient importance to be included in the official announcements.

They were often mere stunts conceived in the brain of sporty staff-officers, whose devotion to the slogan "esprit de corps" served no more useful purpose than to line with corpses the approaches to impossible objectives.

But to the men, who valued their lives and who loved their homes, and who fought because they were told to, or because the exigencies of the moment made them, the raids were feared because they so often represented the narrow margin which separates this life from the next.

CHAPTER IX

THE GERMAN EVACUATION

REST-BILLETS from the frost-bound trenches were situated in the village of Courcelles not far removed from Colincamps, and here we used to recuperate for periods of about four days. It was immune from shell-fire even though batteries were stationed in and around, and although there was no civilian population, we contrived to make ourselves fairly comfortable. The five francs, which was the most a private was allowed to draw in our particular unit, was usually dissipated in the canteen, on candles, chocolate, and cigarettes, and generally the five francs would have to be spent as a whole, for on pay-days the canteen attendants would be overwhelmed with notes, and to ask for change was as good as asking not to be served.

This rigid five-franc maximum was the cause of much discontent, for even if a week was spent in the trenches back pay was never forthcoming. Of course, the difference went to the credit of the individual soldier, but it was small consolation to know that one was piling up credits when one's very existence could not be measured by weeks, or even days.

I know quite well that the men would have preferred

the total amounts that were due, for though they may not have expressed it, their attitude towards life was "Eat, drink, and be merry, for to-morrow ye may die."

These small payments which our troops received contrasted strangely with the pay of the overseas units, and the latter were always more warmly welcomed by the villagers because of the extra purchasing power which they possessed. About the end of the third week in February the thaw set in, and with the commencement of wet weather conditions quickly became intolerable. One night we arrived at Euston dump clad in gumboots, and we found the once hard and slippery communication trench knee-deep in clinging mud. Progress was made with the utmost difficulty. In single file we crept along, dragging first one foot then the other. Halts of long duration were made, and men would curse and rave when they found a leg trapped in a sponge-like substance which no amount of struggling could remove, and many a distracted man unstrapped his gumboots to release himself and continued the journey in his socks. Several long weary hours were occupied on that exhausting march, and the whole route was thickly littered with the implements and attire which had been cast aside in agony.

On the following morning I made a pilgrimage with Shorty down the trench from the supports, and we were astounded with the number of overcoats, ankle boots, gumboots, water-bottles, and trench gloves which were scattered about, in addition to bags of coke and rations in abundance. It testified to the gruelling experience the men had endured, and it was the last time that overcoats were taken into the trenches, for which we were truly thankful.

Overcoats are useful on a cold night, but they are apt to get so saturated and heavy with mud and water that they become a positive encumbrance.

On the second night of this particular period, our gun-team which, by the way, was now led by Shorty, was ordered to report to "B" Company in the front line for work in the posts, and to get there we had to travel the length of the supports and so to the connecting trench. I happened to be taking the lead and, treading on the edge of a duckboard, it suddenly caved in and let me down into a sump at least five feet deep. It is an ill wind that blows nobody any good, and my immersion probably saved someone else, but it was an unpleasant experience, with the prospect of a cold day to follow in the post.

Shorty, the idiot, was grinning, but he assisted me out of the hole and we proceeded to the front line where we found those of the company who were not on duty resting in a dugout. A coke fire was burning brightly and I deliberately stripped to the skin, and commencing with the vest, dried each garment thoroughly, putting on each one as it became dry.

This operation took the greater part of the night, and soon afterwards we heard the voice of the sergeant-major.

"Get dressed, John Cop's post."

Getting dressed, of course, meant getting on equipment.

The words sent a thrill through the waiting men, for they had no desire to leave the comparative warmth and safety of the dugout.

"Fall in, John Cop's post."

We crept up the muddy steps and into the water-logged trench.

"Where's the guide?" someone asks.

"Put that blarsted light out," hisses a sergeant, as a man attempts to light a cigarette.

"Lead on somebody, we shall have it light before we get there."

"Where the hell's the guide? Don't shove, mate, they ain't found the perishing guide yet."

"Christ, ain't it cold; hope Jerry keeps quiet for half-hour."

Then there would be a few moments of silence and the men would stand looking in the direction of the German lines, but we were all impatient to reach the post before the first gleam of daylight appeared, and the hubbub would be renewed.

"Get a move on, will yer."

"Hi, Sergeant! where's the blarsted guide for John Cop's. Ah, here he is. Good old Ernie."

Ernie was a lance-corporal with the eyes of a hawk and a natural sense of direction. He invariably took over the Lewis gun posts in advance of the battalion, and once he had made the journey he remembered the ground to a foot. Some men are born guides and others are not. I, unfortunately, was one of those who were not, and therefore of necessity was compelled to rely upon the superior wisdom of my more gifted comrades.

Ernie took his place at the head.

"Everyone ready?" he asked.

"All ready, Ernie, lead on."

Up and out of the trench we went, splash, splash,

through pools of water, skirting shell-holes and crossing mud channels, slowly, for Ernie was a man with a thought for others. Bending low as a machine-gun swept the front, standing perfectly still when star-shells illuminated the ground, and then on again. Swish—swish, water in every direction, a line of broken willows just discernible in the gloom, a gaunt-looking tree-stump here, a piece of discarded equipment there; little things which spelled the right direction to the man who was leading, and so to the post.

As we approached we saw the gleam of bayonets, and then steel helmets just above the level of the ground. The formality of handing over the position was soon accomplished. It varies according to the locality and the immediate danger. In quiet sectors the relief may be deliberate and unhurried. In lively places no time is wasted. The N.C.O. of the post would immediately get hold of the N.C.O. of the relief and rapidly give instructions. "Here's your front; there's a German machine-gun over there by the three trees. Here's a box of bombs and that's your distress signal. Don't show a finger in daylight. Good night, good luck." Meanwhile, the personnel of the relief would be questioning the relieved as to whether any shelling or bombing took place and what times, and did they drop near, but in any case the whole affair would last but a few seconds, for no man must be seen crossing the open ground after dawn.

John Cop's post also possessed a sap which ran many yards under the ground, but we decided that it would be too unhealthy to all crowd into it. As Shorty put it, "One Jerry at the entrance with a bomb in his hand and we're all candidates for the father-land!"

We were a pretty strong party, for a bombing section under a sergeant had been added to the post, so to make things easier it was mutually decided that a third of the whole should mount guard, leaving the remainder free to smoke or doze, whichever they preferred.

"We've got no grub," said Shorty, as we sat at the entrance of the sap.

"How's that?" I asked.

"'B' Company wouldn't own us for grub. The major said he knew nothing about it and we should have brought it with us."

"That's a damn fine thing, after telling us to ration with 'B' Company," said I. "What are we going to do?"

"I've got a biscuit and some 'Woodbines'," said Shorty.

"So have I," I answered, "but that won't take us far."

It was a peculiar business, this system of rationing. I had experienced it before. Get sent away from your own company or section for a day or even a meal and it was a sure thing that you must starve. No one knows anything about you, and no one seems to care. Sergeants welcome you as an extra help, and keep the ration bag under cover.

"Sorry," says the sergeant-major, "I can't do anything. You'd better see quarters."

"Sorry," says the quartermaster. "I've only indented for the company and it's poor at that." Then, as a final thrust, "Where's your own rations?"

"I've been told to ration with you," you might reply.

"Damn fools! Who told you that?" he answers. You tell him, "Sergeant So-and-So," but it cuts no ice, and you get nothing, and if someone does not take pity on you and give you the back end of a tin of bully to clean out, you go hungry until such time as you can communicate with your own particular people.

That was the position we were in at present, but fortunately the bombing sergeant unearthed a few spare biscuits, and with the addition of the iron rations we were secure for that day, at any rate.

These iron rations which every infantryman carried consisted of a tin of bully, another oval-shaped tin containing tea and sugar, and three biscuits. Where or how the name was derived I know not, but it was certainly appropriate when applied to the biscuits. According to orders they must not be touched until ordinary rations have been missing for forty-eight hours, but only a fool would go short of a meal if he was hungry and felt like tackling the reserve issue. Shorty never hesitated; his emergency tea and sugar rarely came out of a trench with him. He was never satisfied until the oval tin was empty. He preferred it to the ordinary ration any time, and he never got into trouble over it, for Shorty had friends amongst the cooks who religiously refilled the tin as part of their normal duties.

To review the whole of the time spent in that post and alternately in the trenches behind would be so much repetition, and other incidents connecting this part of the front are more worthy of note.

. . . . .

We were again in Courcelles and strange things were

happening. Guns which for months had been firing from pits in the village were being dragged from their positions and hauled along the road to Colincamps. Staff officers could be seen hurrying towards the trenches, and the news spread like wildfire that the Germans were evacuating the line.

The Worcesters moved up to Euston dump.

The few days' interval had produced a remarkable change. Tents were springing up like mushrooms and a road was rapidly being made alongside the old communication trench. We could hardly grasp the fact that it had become perfectly safe to walk about openly when to do so a short time before would have provoked hostile shelling. We spent the night in improvised bivouacs, and for utter discomfort out of the trenches it wanted some beating. The dictionary says that a bivouac is "an encampment of soldiers in the open air". It is. Four of us clubbed together, and with the combined ground-sheets erected something a shade bigger and bulkier than an average-size orange box; only it was not so stout as the much-maligned orange box. We could not make it long enough to accommodate Shorty's legs, and I discovered that night that Shorty in a bivouac was quite a different man to the same person in a comfortable billet. We passed the greater part of the night in constructional work and improvements, and when at last we were ready to get down it was almost time to get up.

Soon after dinner on the following day I was unexpectedly attached to another gun-team and sent to join "B" Company, and not long afterwards we were proceeding in wake of the Germans to the new line.

It was a long trek, past the old posts of bitter memories and on to new ground. There lay one of the men reported missing after the raid of a few Sundays ago. Over the enemy's network of trenches, deserted, but still forbidding, as if they were manned by the ghosts of the army which had gone.

Towards evening we encountered shelling, and passing over a series of light railway tracks we struck a trench which led directly to a position held by a unit whom we were intended to reinforce. The village of Serre lay directly in front of us and was still occupied by the enemy, who were blowing up buildings preparatory to continuing the retreat.

For a couple of days we remained there, always on the *qui vive*, and never sure of what was happening in those trenches opposite, and then just after midnight commenced a long-delayed relief of that sector by a fresh division. We learned with a certain amount of annoyance that the unit charged with the task of taking over our bit of trench had for some reason arrived without its Lewis gunners, and that two men of each gun-team were required to remain behind until they came in. As I was acting as a number two, I naturally came under this category, and was delayed a considerable time in consequence, but finally, the missing gunners arrived and we got away.

The night was now well advanced, and when we reached the light railway track near the end of the trench a strafe commenced of such severity that we ran pell-mell in different directions, and I did not again see my number one on that night. I took shelter for a few minutes for I had no desire to be wounded, alone and in such a desolate place, and when the strafe had ceased I began the long journey back through the wilderness. Fortunately the engineers with astonishing rapidity had laid duckboards along the new route, and finding these by a great stroke of luck, I made rapid progress, and passing John Cop's post, which seemed almost friendly, I presently decided that a rest would be beneficial and accordingly I made a halt in a trench near the duckboards, and sat down.

As it gradually became light I found I was not alone; another man was sitting at the bottom of the trench a few yards away. I walked up to him and saw that he had long since died. Something about his appearance made me think. I looked into his face, which was almost black. It was the face of the man with the heart of gold who had pulled me out of the flooded Somme trench.

I fell to soliloquizing, for I could see myself, sooner or later, sitting in a similar attitude, with blackened face and grinning teeth, and men passing by, saying, "Why don't they bury the poor devil?" and I cursed the war which was stealing my youth, cursed the army and all that it entailed, cursed the bands and the music which had thrilled me, which would always thrill me, and when the mood had passed, I got up and hurried away in the direction of Euston dump.

CHAPTER X

BELGIUM

FROM Bailleul, the road to the line in the spring of 1917 ran through Locre and La Clytte, both places containing most of their normal civilian population. A few kilometres past La Clytte was the deserted village of Dickebusch, and turning to the right a few hundred yards this side of Dickebusch, and keeping the lake on the left, an hour's walk along duckboards would eventually lead to Ridgewood. On the right of the wood lay Kemmel, and only a short distance to the immediate front were the trenches of the Vierstraate sector. We found Ridgewood, which was really a wood, comparatively free from shelling except at regular hours, usually between 9 p.m. and 10 p.m. A supposed armoured train would then drop a few heavies during its nightly tour of the front.

This much being known, it was the general practice for troops occupying the wood to seek shelter in some nearby trenches and return after the load had been delivered. On our first night, adopting the time-honoured precaution, we deserted the huts in the wood, but something went wrong with the usual formula. Either the train was late or the time-table had been suddenly altered. We endured a weary wait until nearly midnight, and then, somewhat sceptical, began to converge on the more congenial shelter of the huts. Of course, at this precise moment the overdue shells arrived, and there was a stampede for the trench. Subsequently, the train, if it was a train, kept to its correct time and caused no further anxiety in that respect.

We spent several days in the woods, and it was here that I learned to make and enjoy that curious concoction known as trench-pudding.

This consisted of broken biscuits, and currants, which occasionally came up in the rations, boiled with a covering of water until they were a pulpy mess, the resultant mixture being devoured with a relish which was a fair commentary on our perverted tastes.

The Lewis guns had now been distributed amongst the companies and, together with Shorty and Mark, I found myself permanently attached to "D" Company.

The Vierstraate trenches which we took over in due course were a revelation to those of us who had been reared on the Somme. They had been defended during two and a half years of war, and were modelled on generous and even comfortable lines. Small splinter-proof shelters were built into the sides of the trench and there were sufficient of these to accommodate the whole of the men who were holding the line.

Timbered and revetted, and with a perfect drainage system, it was possible for men to polish their boots and keep them clean. That they were directly under the observation of the enemy was beyond dispute, for the Germans occupied the crest of the famous ridge from which could be obtained a clear and uninterrupted view of the British lines. Why they did not methodically batter the trenches was a mystery, and the only solution I could find was that the sector was a resting-place for troops who had endured the rigours of the more lively parts of the front.

Vierstraate was not to be confused as a health resort by any means, for strafes took place occasionally and men died there as they did elsewhere. Snipers, too, were much in evidence and offered a likely target; they fired but once and rarely missed.

Our first spell in the line was almost devoid of incident. So quiet was the neighbourhood during the greater part of the time that it was hard to realize we were standing on the doorstep of the war. Birds could be heard singing, and with the glorious sun of a spring morning the deception was complete. This state of affairs was evidently too tame for our superiors, and orders were issued for buttons to be cleaned, but we were becoming old soldiers and cleaning tackle had been left behind. Shaving was compulsory, however, and this was easily possible, for a shell was a rarity and consequently our nerves suffered little. We were never allowed to remain idle for long. Afternoons only were devoted to rest, and nights and mornings spent in improving the trenches, especially in the sand-bagging of the front line. If there was no work it was created by stripping the bottom of the trench and cleaning the muck from underneath. The higher officers had work, for others, on the brain. You could not move a couple of yards without being detailed to do this or that.

Generally speaking, however, we had what one might call a fairly good time considering that we were in the trenches, and we held high hopes that our sojourn on that part of the front would be indefinite, but contrary to our expectations we were withdrawn and commenced another series of daily marches which culminated in the sleepy little village of Acquin some three miles from the better-known Lumbries on the main St. Omer-Boulogne road.

Here we were billeted in fairly comfortable though drafty barns. "D" company was thrust wholesale into the farm-buildings of a French farmer with whom we quickly became on the best of terms.

The company barber shaved him daily and the medical officer attended the minor ailments of his children, and a spirit was engendered which was reflected in the sing-songs which took place nightly in the farmer's kitchen.

We did our best to milk the cows, gave the pigs the residue of dried vegetable and bully stew, drew the water from the well, and last but not least, discovered where the fowls laid. This latter achievement belonged exclusively to Shorty. He came to Mark and myself bearing an air of mystery.

"I say, you chaps," he whispered. "Come with me; I've found the goods."

We followed him to the back of the house where we saw a couple of fair-sized fowl-houses.

"The nests," said Shorty, with a smirk.

There was the usual little aperture for the fowls to enter, and he made a preliminary reconnaissance with his arm, but found that he was short of the desired objects.

"What we want is a soup ladle," said he.

"How about a jam tin on a stick," suggested Mark.

That idea seemed worth trying, and we adjourned to the barn, presently returning singly and by diverse routes. The jam tin was securely fastened to the stick and, with a dexterity which was amazing, Shorty began hooking eggs out of the nests.

We had eggs for breakfast, eggs for supper, and eggs beat up in tea for want of a better use, and then one day Mark, whose turn it was to fetch these extra rations, was nearly surprised by the farmer, and in his hurry to get away he left the jam tin in the nest.

Presently, howls of execration came from the irate Frenchman, who was prancing about the yard brandishing the jam tin, and accusing everyone within reach of being the cause of his shortage of eggs.

"Serve the old fool right," was Shorty's comment. "I've seen enough issue 'bacca and tins of bully in his cupboard to last him till the war's over."

Shorty was undoubtedly right, for it was not an uncommon thing for villagers to have in their possession stocks of army rations which could not have been acquired openly.

Scrounging, as it was called, had certainly been brought to a fine art, and Shorty was a past-master at the game.

On one occasion we were billeted in barns which directly faced the windows of the farmer's dwelling, and if this particular farmer had never seen the Worcesters before, he had seen their kith and kin, and by the precautions he took he did not trust them. He locked up his fowls each night and set a ferocious dog on guard.

The dog did not like khaki and we did not like the dog, and between us there raged a perpetual feud.

We used to eat our meals outside the barn and the fowls had a kindly habit of strutting about waiting for luscious worms, which we threw to them, in the form of bits of stringy meat.

It had got to come, as everyone knew, and, of course, it was Shorty who evolved the plan, and executed it. One day, just after dinner had been issued and the men were sitting about with steaming canteens, he told us not to throw anything to the birds; so we didn't. He then turned the large dixie on its side with the opening facing us and away from the house. Presently, with many "cluck clucks", the fowls surrounded it and two or three walked inside to do business on the scraps.

Shorty was as cool as the proverbial cucumber, and seeing that the coast was clear, he clapped on the lid and then bawled out for someone to assist him with the dixie back to the field-kitchen. It was carried out so rapidly that I doubt even if the farmer and his household had been watching they would have suspected that anything was amiss. The cooks were in the scheme, naturally, and it was a merry little party that supped off chicken that night.

These shady doings may seem immoral, but then war is immoral, and men living in an atmosphere of war lose touch with the finer points of life and do things which in the honest atmosphere of civilian life they would condemn. I personally joined whole-heartedly in such schemes, and in the dead of night I have raided potato buries and apple trees, and enjoyed the exploits and thought what a fine time I was having, and I never considered for a moment that there was anything wrong in it. I doubt if the French farmers lost anything in proportion to what they gained, for the billets had to be paid for, halfpenny per head per night, I was led to understand, and a barn which could accommodate fifty or more troops was a paying proposition. This, in addition to the money which changed hands for coffee, bread, and (quietly) little drops of cognac. Never did I see any sign of resentment on the part of the farming community when a company of men were thrust on them; and even amongst the peasants who worked the land the same spirit was manifest. The man, if he was above military age, or otherwise not liable for service, would return home from the fields in the evening and find his cottage overrun with troops, and he would settle down in some corner and eat his meal fully content with the knowledge that madame was doing a roaring trade in eggs and chips at a franc and a half a plate, and mademoiselle, the elder daughter, perspiring with the exertion of making coffee, would change five-franc notes with a rapidity that proved such contingences had been well provided for.

In the countryside around Acquin intense field training was undergone and many sham advances staged. This caused not a little concern, for it was an understood fact that training of this character was provided only when a "push" was in project.

Vimy Ridge had just been captured by the Canadians and the whole front was beginning to pulsate with movement.

For the purpose of these mock battles, the barrage was represented by signallers equipped with flags, who would walk slowly forward at a speed corresponding to the movement of an actual barrage.

We heard of some startling innovations which caused much heated discussion among the men.

A new form of attack was practised, in this manner: Three lines of trenches were to be stormed, and the first wave, instead of overcoming the first line, was to push on, under protection of the barrage, cross the second line before the defenders could get out of the dugouts, and so to the third line, which they would capture and consolidate. The second wave would follow and capture the German second line, and the third wave the first line. Lewis guns would be in the first wave, their task being to push on through lanes provided by the barrage and establish outposts in front of the whole.

In billets that night we held an inquest on this brain-wave of our superiors.

"What a rotten idea," said Mark. "What happens to us if the second wave gets held up?"

"Dear Mother, on postcards showing the German Eagle," I suggested.

"We shall never see the third line," said Shorty. "We'll be shot in the back for a pound, but that ain't the point. What about this infernal lane in the barrage that we've got to find? Can you chaps spot a lane in a barrage?"

It was problematical.

"Can't be done," said Mark. "The blighters who invented it ought to try it."

"They had that," Shorty answered vehemently. "It would put a stop to their idiotic ideas."

We argued long and earnestly.

It was all very well in theory, but we knew in practice it would turn out otherwise. A barrage of advancing shells might be comforting, but it was also awe-inspiring, and sometimes a few dropped short, and sometimes the enemy sent a counter barrage which mingled with our own so that it was impossible to tell what was happening. As Mark put it, unless our shells had Union Jacks on them it would be a washout.

Thankful we were that the powers saw the errors of their ways, and in our brigade, at least, we were never called upon to attempt such suicidal tactics.

CHAPTER XI

THE SALIENT AND HILL 60

ONCE again we set our faces in the direction of the line, and soon we were in the neighbourhood of Poperinghe, where the troops for the Ypres sector usually collected. These long journeys were accomplished by stages of from fifteen to twenty kilometres daily, and with an early start we were generally in billets early in the afternoon.

The procedure was invariably the same.

The orderly sergeant would come round the last thing at night and read out orders for the ensuing day. "Reveille, five-thirty. Breakfast, six o'clock. Blankets to be rolled in bundles of tens and taken to the transport lines. Parade, seven o'clock, full marching order." At the time stated, the battalion would march off in column of route, headed by the band, and followed by the field kitchens and transport, and every fifty minutes a ten minutes' halt would be called, when the troops would line the route and secure what little rest was possible.

Towards midday, if the breeze was in a certain direction, a smell of stew would begin to emanate from the field kitchens, for meals would be prepared beforehand and cooked on the march, and at dinner-time we would halt for an hour and storm the dixies which the mess orderlies had fetched.

Then the last stages of the march would be resumed, and the men would begin to ask each other how much blarsted farther it was, and if the colonel on his horse knew where he was going. Packs would be hitched up higher and ordinary conversation cease.

Each village that hove in sight was hailed with delight as the end of the journey; but as we marched through, at attention, envious glances would be cast at the soldiers who lined the road curious to see which unit was ours.

"Eyes right," to a turned-out guard, and then out into the open country again.

Some men would obviously be getting weary. Occasionally a man would step aside to await the oncoming limbers and a certain "crime" if he was only tired. A few scattered farms and houses would appear ahead. The band would strike up the regimental march. The troops would straighten their backs and walk erect. The billets were in sight.

The morning after our arrival at Poperinghe I was selected with two other Lewis gunners to accompany an officer to the trenches for a preliminary review of the posts. A motor-bus, typical of the everyday life of London and packed with an assortment of bombers, signallers, and gunners from various units, carried us along the La Clytte road to the outskirts of Dickebusch. Here a fierce strafe was taking place and the driver flatly refused to take his bus any further, so we descended, and making a detour to avoid the shelling, proceeded on foot towards Ypres.

A turn to the right was made in the suburbs of the

famous city, and following the canal and then the railway line, we passed the dugouts in the embankment, and finally entered a communication trench near Transport farm. This led us to the front line, where we found the King's Own Yorkshire Light Infantry, the unit we were due to relieve. Meals were supplied by the cooks, and I discovered that the system for serving hot meals in the trenches had been brought by this battalion to the highest state of perfection. The officers and men bore an air of coolness and contentment which was refreshing in view of the unenviable reputation which the Salient had justly gained.

In the evening a jovial sergeant proposed a walk to the posts, and we were about to don our equipment when he stopped us.

"Leave that stuff here," he said. "I never reckon to carry anything but a couple of Mills, you do the same."

We readily agreed, for the heavy equipment was a bane at the best of times, and with a bomb in each trousers pocket we followed the sergeant along the trench. It was a pudding-bag trench with a dead end jutting towards the enemy lines; and climbing out, we skirted the remains of a wood and came to the first post.

Looking back, I saw an extraordinary sight. We were at the apex of the Salient, and Verey lights appeared almost behind as well as in front. Only a narrow bottle-neck between the lines of lights denoted the path to safety. Shelling of the rear lines was taking place, the heavy missiles passing high over our heads to explode in or near the city beyond, and overhead machine-gun fire was so terrific that it appeared wellnigh impossible for anything to live.

I had the curious feeling that the safest spot on the whole of the Salient was Lone Tree Post, where we were then resting. After a cursory inspection of the other posts, we returned to the trench, and in a little iron shelter I slept as soundly and peacefully as I did in the straw-covered barn at Acquin. The next evening the battalion arrived. They had marched the greater part of the distance wearing respirators, for the warning of gas had been received *en route*, but it was strange that in the trenches we knew nothing about it.

Being new-comers to this sector our officers immediately began to take the extraordinary precautions which a battalion does take when first occupying a strange part of the front. The coolness and contentment of the outgoing unit went with them and a feeling of restlessness prevailed. Sleep was banned and sentries trebled and preparations made as though an attack was imminent. However, little shelling took place for the first few hours, and as shelling is the supreme factor for "nerves" in the trenches, the comparative absence of such had a wonderful effect in bolstering the spirits of the timid. With the dawn and the warmth of the sun, everyone decided that the Salient was not such a bad old place after all. So much for that. The ensuing day did not realize the hopes of the previous night, and I append here extracts from a letter which I had the audacity to send to my brother, in a green envelope.

It is dated 4th April, 1917.

"I am now basking in the sunshine somewhere around Ypres. . . . To express myself correctly I should have to say it is a bloody place, in both senses.

Fritz is all around us and can shell us when and where he likes. . . . Just as I had written this he commenced to strafe us with 'coalboxes', and I have been crawling about the trench with this letter in my hand expecting my number to go up every second. It is still on, but I have entrenched myself behind an empty biscuit tin, hoping for the best. Our batteries have opened now and shells are going over like paddle-steamers. I hope Fritz is having his tea. . . ."

Yes, our premature conception of the Salient was wrong, radically wrong, and in a very short time we were hoping and praying for the relief. Our prayers were answered, in a fashion, for on the third day we moved into the unhealthy atmosphere of Hill 60. "D" Company went in the supports, a trench nice and dry but too wide to be called safe.

We were separated from the front line by a very narrow piece of trench but a few yards in length, and one or two enthusiasts were soon exploring the immediate neighbourhood. I walked up the narrow communication, finding on the way an enormous shell which was lying unexploded and partially buried in the earth. I was in the front line, which held only a handful of men, before I imagined I was anywhere near, and the occupants with pantomimic gestures bade me keep quiet as the Germans were only fifteen yards away. Indeed, my intrusion was so resented that I quickly cleared out and returned to the supports. The trenches of Hill 60 seemed to smell of death, and well they might, for hundreds of gallant men lay underneath those heaped-up masses of torn earth.

The hill, if hill it could be called—it was really little more than a slope—was a maze of wrecked trenches and craters, each gaping hole bearing silent witness to the tortures of the unhappy past.

We endured days of hell, each day producing its full complement of fresh horrors of chaos and frightfulness. Minnenwerfers or "oil drums", as we called them, kept us in a constant state of nerves. The first suspicion we had of "Minnies" was a fearful crash which rocked the trench. Then a strange, unfamiliar gurgling noise and another crash and the cry of a wounded man. Looking up, we could see a huge cylindrical projectile wobbling down rapidly from above. Now the dance with death commenced in earnest. Dashing along the trench, now backwards, now forwards, colliding with each other to escape the terror, clenching teeth and sweating with fear, cursing and praying alternately, with shouts of bomb right and bomb left only adding to the confusion.

Nothing was comparable to the havoc of a "Minnie". It would obliterate a traverse, but fortunately its descent could be watched and to a certain extent the position of its fall calculated. With more than one "Minnie" in the air at one time speculation was of little use, but happily the majority of them would miss the actual trench, otherwise our casualties would have been very large indeed.

A diversion occurred one afternoon when British and German planes were engaged in a fierce duel overhead, the outcome of which was that a German machine was forced down in flames to drop not fifty yards from where we were entrenched. The desire of certain individuals to run to the burning machine was sternly repressed, and with good reasons, for the enemy artillery opened with such ferocity that the machine was ultimately battered to pieces, and that regardless of the possibility that the pilot may have been still alive.

On the night that we were to be relieved the enemy attempted a raid, but so terrific was our own barrage that the attempt failed at the onset.

Later we filed out of those horrible trenches, and here and there men carried with them sandbags which contained parts of the mortal remains of those who were once their comrades.

At midnight we reached the railway dugouts. They were commodious and fitted with bunks of wire netting, and soon all were comfortably sleeping. Exactly six hours later we were rudely awakened and the majority of us hustled off to Ypres on a working party. This was a most unusual occurrence, for the first day following a spell in the line was almost invariably spent in rest and cleaning up.

All day we worked in the stricken city, loading trucks with the bricks of demolished buildings, and pushing the trucks far on the way to Dickebusch, and on our return to the dugouts we found that they had been reduced to heaps of debris, and of the men who were left behind, some forty were killed and wounded But for that providential working-party the battalion would have been a battalion in name only.

I availed myself of the opportunity of visiting the huge cemetery not far away. Here lay the Canadians who were gassed in the early part of 1915:—whole companies lying side by side, victims of the most devilish invention of man.

Near to the cemetery was the improvised mortuary, and I was deeply shocked to see the labelled bodies of men whom I had so recently known. There, too, were the gruesome sandbags, each with its ticket bearing name and number, familiar names. So insignificant taking the brutal war as a whole; so overwhelming from an individual standpoint.

Strong men, full of life, of love. Men who had embarked on the great adventure with hope and faith and confidence; had conceived the joys of peace and the reunion of home ties, and had entered on, perhaps without knowing it, that sleep from which there is no awakening.

Poor victims of the war lords.

I heard the tramp of feet, the burial parties, but I had no heart to see more.

Working parties now became our lot. On one occasion we carried timber to the front line near Hooge, to be used in the mining operations which were being pushed forward. Three journeys were made, and small or big, strong or weak, each had to carry the same weight, and many a little David staggered along with the burden of a Goliath.

Even men who were physically incapable of carrying heavy loads must do the journeys or collapse by the wayside, for there is no mercy in war.

How we hated the engineer officer or sergeant who had charge of those working parties, and yet it was but their duty that they performed. They were personally responsible for the delivery of the material which we handled, but no excuse would mitigate the offence of their authority, in the eyes of the perspiring infantryman. On another occasion a certain dump was to be reached where instructions would be given us as to the work required. Just as we were nearing the dump something must have happened in the line, for a terrific volume of machine-gun fire broke out, soon to be followed by the whole concentrated fire of the batteries covering the Salient. We seemed to be the only troops in that quarter, for not another soul was to be seen. Amid the inferno could be distinguished the whistling of countless bullets, and not knowing whether they were high or low, friendly or otherwise, we decided to man an adjacent trench and prepare for eventualities. None of us knew the locality, and we appeared to be in the centre of a half-circle of hundreds of furnace doors which opened and shut and belched forth fire.

The situation was certainly embarrassing, and after a couple of hours of it we decided to find the nearest way to billets.

Such was life in that sector, and such it had been in varying measure since the early days of the war. Troops who in their turn held the gate of the Salient held the gate of hell and, happily, held it successfully.

The Worcesters marched away feeling like men reprieved, and at Shrapnel Corner, where there happened to be a block in the traffic, the Germans sent the last few shells, which burst near enough to put new life into tired limbs. A train was waiting on the outskirts of Ypres, a dilapidated French passenger train but welcome nevertheless, and in perfect darkness and almost without a sound, we steamed away from the skeleton city, and so to Poperinghe.

CHAPTER XII

VIERSTRAATE

NEAR to Locre on the main Bailleul Road were cross-roads known officially as Canada Corner, and on a piece of ground which formed half of a square, or better still, an angle, for the two sides abutted the cross-roads, lay a number of huts where for fully a fortnight we resided.

In Locre could be found good cheer and amusement, and in numerous other villages within easy distance enjoyment was to be obtained.

But such was not for us. The whole of the battalion, with the exception of the band and certain other lucky mortals, was being employed as working parties in the Vierstraate sector, and promptly at seven o'clock each evening we marched to the line, arriving there about ten.

Our task was the making of a trench behind the support line, with a parapet strong enough to withstand the heaviest shells, and for this purpose large numbers of sandbags were filled, a job which necessitated many holes being dug elsewhere to ensure an adequate supply of earth.

The troops were always tired after the long march from Canada Corner, and a couple of hours' sandbag-filling was not calculated to inspire energy. Men would curl up in the holes and go to sleep, and it was a common sight to see the sergeants waking the chaps up to come home. One of them suggested that Reveille should be blown to ease matters.

A great change had taken place in this once quiet and peaceful sector. Guns were being brought up to forward positions and camouflaged to avoid detection. Roads were being constructed as near to the line as possible, and as each piece was completed it was cunningly concealed with turf and brushwood.

Light railway tracks had been pushed up to within measurable distance of the support line, all these preparations indicating an advance at an early date.

Four hours was the stipulated length of time which we were supposed to work, and the amount got through by a whole company would have been despised by any self-respecting gang of navvies. Perhaps this factor was recognized by the authority responsible for the work, and remedied by the simple expedient of calling for double the number of men actually required.

Following our return to the huts we would prepare for an inspection of rifles and chins, and then do an hour's drill under the sergeant-major, who had not done the march to the line and back again. After that, providing there was nothing more to be done, we might sleep, or write home, or even visit the estaminets of Locre, but the touching part about this business was that the troops were so fatigued with the double journey that all interest in the material side of life was lacking, and we lived from day to day with the single hope that each journey would be the last.

This happy state of affairs was eventually realized. The working parties finished and there was much joy and thanksgiving, and we then moved into the support line.

An even greater change was to be noted there. Gone was the serene quietness which had characterized our earlier visit, and no longer did the birds chirp to the glories of spring mornings, for almost continuously the British batteries were pouring shells into the German trenches and rear lines, and the enemy, alarmed and outraged, often replied with devastating effect. The support line was a good trench as previously described, but the little iron shelters, so lightly protected with sandbags, were worse than useless against direct shell-bursts.

At one point, near where the communication trench led to the front line, there was a loop, and large numbers of these shelters had been erected on a comparatively small piece of ground. Soon after "stand down" on the first night the Germans began a hot bombardment of the trench with guns of a very heavy calibre. The loop was given special attention and the shelters were quickly blown to pieces. Much panic occurred among the occupants, who fortunately at the very commencement decided to quit that portion of the line. They swelled through the ranks of "D" Company with wild staring eyes, some showing all the symptoms of shell-shock when they desperately attempted to tear up the duckboards at the bottom of the trench to seek shelter beneath.

One man with distorted face was shrieking, "There's thousands of dead down there."

For an hour the great shells continued to burst,

throwing up columns of earth which descended on us in volumes and scattering widely pieces of jagged iron capable of tearing a man in halves. But when the strafe had subsided it was discovered that the casualties were not so heavy as might have been expected, for most of the shells had exploded in or near the vacated trench, which had been completely demolished. Several men were wounded and one killed outright. He had received the full force of a shell-burst, for only particles of his body could be found, and although there was barely sufficient to bury, a grave was made and some time later a wooden cross was erected to his memory. Three days were spent in the supports, then "D" Company moved into the front line where we immediately became subjected to a strafe of "Minnies", but I had the satisfaction of watching through a periscope a similar medicine administered to the Germans with the Stokes trench mortar.

The huge footballs were dropping right into the enemy front line, and the explosions which followed must have caused something more than uneasiness to the defenders. Trench mortars were a good asset, but they were strongly objected to by the infantry. The operators had a nasty habit of firing half a dozen rounds and then clearing out as speedily as possible. Generally, the spot from where they had fired would become the centre of a strafe and the troops would have a warm half an hour.

We liked the Stokes, but preferred it at a distance. The fire of the British batteries was increasing daily, and now and again developed into a fierce bombardment. Fresh guns were continually registering targets, and it was very evident that something big was about to take place.

This persistent shelling was a source of great worry to us, for it provoked the enemy to reply, and his reply was usually directed at the trenches.

"Why can't they leave the swines alone?" a man would remark, and that seemed to be the general opinion. Leave him alone, and perhaps he will leave us alone. This was purely a personal opinion, and it would certainly have been a foolish policy considering that the very nature of the shelling was reducing the *morale* of the enemy and making easier the imminent advance. Unfortunately we could only look on the position from one standpoint; our lives were being endangered, for even though a man may be counted a mere atom of an army at war, he is still a man with the desire to live, and he instinctively loathes the factor which tends to cut short his puny existence.

British aeroplanes were much in evidence at this period, and had gained a superiority over the enemy which was refreshing. The rival air forces seemed to take turns in being mistress of the air. Sometimes for days the Germans would fly unchallenged, and then the British would introduce a new type of machine and quickly regain the title.

On the evening of the first day in the front line we heard semi-officially that an aeroplane scout had reported enemy troops massing on our front. Such warning was not to be taken light-heartedly and preparations made accordingly.

Shorty busied himself with the gun, oiling it, fondling it, and even talking to it.

"Yes, my precious," he was saying, his face beaming with exultation, "we'll give 'em massing, won't we?

"You and me knows what to do if they gets poking their ugly noses round here. Get them bombs ready, you chaps, and don't get dropping the blinking pins out."

Mark was superintending the loosening of the pins and, as they were got ready, they were placed on the firestep, where they formed an imposing array. I had collected all the available Verey lights, and was instructed by Shorty to start "shooting daylight" directly it became too dark to see the immediate front. The batteries which had been firing throughout the day began to cease with the approach of dusk, and every man was alert, with his rifle handy and a bullet up the breech to start with.

For several hours we remained thus and during that time quite a large number of star-shells were fired from different parts of the trench, and I had learned, at the expense of burnt eyebrows, that the proper way to hold a Verey light pistol was at arm's length. Now, as a general rule, the British left the lighting up of "No Man's Land" almost wholly to the enemy, for we were able to see as much as we desired with the number of lights he disposed of.

Whether the Germans thought that we were discharging so many fireworks as a feint for a subsequent attack will never be known, but at any rate a barrage was directed on "D" company.

The earlier warning of a possible assault defined this barrage as the prelude, and a distress signal was fired. The batteries responded at once, and all together, and the enemy, quite aware that an advance on our part was to be expected at any moment, fired his distress signals along a good stretch of front. All the elements of a local battle were now in progress. "D" company, as one man, was discharging rifles as quickly as the triggers could be pulled, and bomb after bomb was thrown to check the invaders, while at precisely the same time the enemy was firing heavily and throwing bombs for the same purpose.

The "battle" did not last long, however, but as a grande finale, and just about the time when the enemy had decided to waste no more ammunition on sham fights, we fired "fifteen rounds rapid", with Lewis gun accompaniment, to which one solitary German replied by discharging his Verey light pistol point-blank at the trench. The next night a raid on a small scale was organized with the object of obtaining a prisoner for interrogation. Preceded by a ten minutes' strafe, one officer and two men made the attempt, and the astonishing part about it was that not a shot was fired in defence. We saw the men disappear into the German front line, and a few minutes later they returned, escorting two prisoners. It seemed to prove that the enemy had withdrawn, leaving but a few men with plenty of star-shells to delude us into believing that the defence was up to strength.

The break of day was often accompanied by a rolling mist, and gas alarms were of frequent occurrence. Early one morning we were "standing to", and just as a working party of the South Wales Borderers was passing through the trench on their way to the rear the dreaded word "gas" was sounded along the line. Instantly "tin hats" were flung off and gas-masks donned, a feat which was performed quicker than it takes to write, for we thoroughly believed in the oft-repeated maxim that in a gas attack there were but two kinds of men—the quick and the dead.

Shorty was standing on the firestep making a speech which was badly muffled by his respirator.

"Here it comes, boys! Phosgene, by the look of it. We shall just get the tail end. The boys on the left will get it thick. Keep your masks on."

And then the mist, which we had firmly believed was a gas cloud, rolled gradually away. The South Wales Borderers took off their masks and picked up their "tin hats" and passed on, and we took off our masks and picked up our hats and stayed where we were, and when it had become properly light some of us were pained to discover the letters "S.W.B." painted on our hats.

Some form of excitement was always present, yet the hours would pass with painful slowness and the days of the week would become so muddled that I was uncertain whether it was Tuesday or Thursday. The incessant thunder of the guns was horribly trying to the nerves, a particular worry being the ear-splitting crash of a 60-pounder battery which kept going hard and fast for hours on end

Fortunately the weather was nice and warm and the trench dry enough to lie in, and many long spells did I put in on the bottom of the trench vainly trying to interest myself in the *Weekly Dispatch*, and hoping that each shell which burst near was not the beginning of another strafe.

It was quite impossible to feel contented in such an atmosphere of violent shocks. One was always apprehensive of the ensuing night or the coming day, and there were few men who were not painfully conscious of the limitations of their pluck, yet somehow they managed to preserve that attitude of apparent calmness which, after all, is the hall-mark of quiet courage.

CHAPTER XIII

BEHIND THE LINE

TOWARDS the end of May, 1917, the Worcesters were under canvas in pleasant surroundings just a short distance from the village of Westhoutre and some two kilometres off the Bailleul-Ypres road.

The craze for button-cleaning and pack and equipment scrubbing had developed into a mania. Daily inspections were something to be dreaded by the man who had omitted any detail affecting his personal appearance. "C.B." in large and frequent doses was the order of the day, and the mournful notes of the prisoners' bugle-call, "Defaulters, at the double", was answered with the scurrying of many feet.

The provost-sergeant, a one-time prize-fighter, was doing a roaring business and enjoying it, and on his none too innocent head was poured the silent curses of a multitude of delinquents.

On parade, the battalion sparkled with brightness and polish, and if victory had rested on "Soldiers' Friend" and "Blanco", it would have been ours without more ado. The badge of the Worcestershire Regiment was emblazoned on our helmets and, therefore, in future the enemy would have no difficulty in identifying his opponents, should they be lying out after a stunt.

Under the category of cleanliness shirts took second place. True, we had shower-baths and changes of underclothing at varying periods, but even the sterilizing process did not rid the washing of all the parasites which clung to it, and a few days after a clean change men would be seen half-stripped carrying on the never-ending war of extermination. I had long since lost my nausea for such minor details. For the first few weeks I had kept moderately clean by carrying three sets of underclothing and changing and washing them every second day, but I soon discovered the necessity for reducing the weight to be carried, and directly I had dumped the extra garments I became the same as the others, and had been so ever since, and knew quite well that I could not hope for anything better until the war was over, or I got back to England as a casualty.

Thus it came about that the cleanliness of a battalion on parade extended no farther than the brightness of the buttons and the polish of the leather.

I was becoming accustomed to the habit of war. Ordinarily a clean-minded and peaceably-disposed citizen, I hardly noticed that a marked change was taking place in my attitude towards life. I was, perhaps unconsciously, becoming akin to the beasts of the field. I could sit by the side of a corpse long since dead and scrape out a tin of pork-and-beans with evident relish. The instinct of self-preservation was developed to the full. Life was sometimes horrible, but life was sweet, and I wanted to live. The sight of the bloody wounds of other men was revolting, but while I escaped and continued to escape I was more than satisfied.

I had no room for the creed of fatalism in my soul: that fallacy of when your time has come it has come, that a man has but a definite number of days to live and no more. I believed that if a man could miss a point of danger he was missing a chance of death. And what of the followers of the creed of fatalism? Were they so imbued with their belief that they could take unnecessary risks, knowing that if their time had not come they would be perfectly safe from death? Not a bit of it! The shells which unnerved me unnerved them; they feared the stunts, the trenches, and the working parties, just as much as I did. Fatalism was a fake, a kind of a fairy god-thought to impose on the tortured mind and tell it not to be frightened, it was quite all right.

I was struck with the dual characters around me. Here and there a bullying N.C.O., who would crime a man for next to nothing; who behaved as though the possession of one, two, or three stripes was divine dispensation; who collared the biggest share of the rations, if he had the slightest chance; who was a soldier out of the line and a cringing coward in. Fortunately, he was in the minority, but he was to be found, nevertheless. And then the cursing, blaspheming private whose every second word was lurid or filthy; who would steal the loop of his comrade's jack-knife and in the line would call on the God he had abused for mercy. He, too, was in the minority, but could be found.

It is only to be expected that in a war so great, in which such huge numbers of men were engaged, that all classes and characters must be brought together. The rich and poor, the cultured and illiterate were intermingled, and discovered in each other traits which led to a mutual understanding. Friendships were made that would have endured but for the inevitable toll of war.

The face of an infantry battalion was constantly changing. Death, sickness, and wounds necessitated constant drafts to keep it up to a useful strength. Men came one day, hovered around the war-zone for a week or a month, and then passed on to hospital or oblivion. Over a period of twelve months a unit might easily have a couple of thousand soldiers on its roll and yet never muster more than six hundred at any given time. This ebb and flow of man-power applied equally to officers as it did to the rank and file. The casualties among subalterns was enormous, but among the higher ranks it was reduced by withholding the officers from some of the stunts which were likely to prove costly. This method was extended to the senior non-commissioned officers, and a sergeant usually became temporary sergeant-major for the purposes of an attack.

Of all the officers I served under none interested me more than the second-lieutenant who controlled the platoon during our stay at Westhoutre. He was quite an elderly man, perhaps bordering on fifty, rather short and thin, and sharp-featured. He was always on the move, generally in a bustle, and as fussy as a man could be. His pet aversion was to see dirt in a certain little hole in the mechanism of the rifle, and he would go off "the deep end" immediately his keen eyes detected the merest atom of dust.

Naturally, we administered the medicine he liked and cleaned out the little hole especially for his benefit, although one man who hailed from Walsall took the greatest delight in deliberately filling up the very hole which was the bone of contention.

"It's the maker's hole, sir," he would say.

"It does not matter whose hole it is, it has got to be cleaned," the officer would reply, and between these two a conversation of a similar nature took place almost daily.

He would never "crime" a man without the greatest provocation. He would prefer to talk to him in a fatherly manner and point out the error of his ways. When he first joined us we wondered how the dickens he had managed to get so far into the war and what in the world brought him to the infantry, but Lieutenant Sprig quickly won our admiration by his courage and good nature.

He thought a great deal of his platoon and, during the short time he was with us, he made it his especial business to see that we never went into the line without cigarettes. Time after time, when we have been ready to move away, he has come along, accompanied by his servant, carrying several boxes of "Woodbines", which he has proceeded to distribute to each individual under his charge.

He was brave to the point of recklessness. On one occasion, in a rather warm part of the line, his servant, for some unexplained reason, threw over the parapet a cup which belonged to the officer. Lieutenant Sprig immediately climbed out and had just recovered it when a sniper obligingly put a bullet through the side of his steel helmet. He coolly stood there and was actually taking off his hat to examine it when the servant rudely pulled him back into the trench. The officer prized that helmet and, I believe, I am correct in recording that he wrote to the War Office with a view to purchase, and that that benevolent institution charged him twelve shillings and sixpence for the privilege of keeping it.

Periodically we had church parades in the form of a drum-head service. It was a parade which was compulsory, and it afforded an opportunity for much "swanking" of the battalion. An orgy of "forming fours" and "dressing by the right" preceded and followed it, the actual service being a minor event compared with military etiquette. I often considered how much better it would be if such services were voluntary and those who wished to worship could do so without the fear of incurring the displeasure of sergeant-majors and their retinues. Some of the drills performed at Westhoutre were those of a peace-time army, and of all movements the slow march was the most ridiculous. It was as ludicrous as the much-criticized German "goose-step". It made ordinary privates like myself think that we ought to lose the war. Conceived originally by the Guards, it became the chief amusement of the senior officers of many other battalions, and they gloried in it.

The weather was fine, and the camp a model of what a camp should be. Parades usually ended at about half-past three, and after tea had been issued a general exodus would be made to the village. It was an enterprising little place, whose inhabitants catered for the troops and enriched themselves immensely by so doing. Estaminets would be filled to overflowing, and the choruses of popular songs would re-echo through the streets.

Tommy out of the trenches was no sentimentalist. He drank his beer or his coffee with gusto, and called for more. He chatted with Madame and flirted with Mademoiselle. He bought silk postcards and sent them home to Maud and Anne, and he contrived to cram into an evening the pleasures of a week. A man could sit from six o'clock until eight and be quite happy and comfortable on less than half a franc. Not that everyone went to the estaminets. Some preferred the wholesome atmosphere of the villagers' houses and enjoyed the inevitable eggs and chips.

Occasionally, in the camp, the divisional band would give a concert, and men would heartily sing, "You'd be far better off in a home", and the band conductor, a stoutish jovial man, would dance about and wave his stick, and they would sing louder and laugh merrier and feel the better for it.

At seven o'clock each evening the buglers sounded "Tattoo", and immediately afterwards the drums and fifes would commence a series of tunes and marches, which seemed to hold an irresistible fascination for those who had preferred to stay in camp.

It impressed me greatly. Even in after years it would produce that curious feeling, that reaching back of the mind to scenes that were for ever sacred. It produced that insatiable desire to revisit the battlefields, to commune, as it were, with the spirits of the dead. The call of the Somme and of Flanders must for ever be in the blood of those who suffered there.

We were rapidly approaching the time which was to be the culminating point of all the preparations that had taken place on the immediate front. Rehearsal of the method of attack had been carried out, and a model of the enemy trenches facing Vierstraate had been prepared and explained.

The duty of the Worcesters was to push through the first and second lines, after they had been previously captured by other units, and assault the third position, known as the Black Line.

The programme was not received with the enthusiasm which newspapers would have people believe. We knew perfectly well that in front of those trenches of Vierstraate lay defences which had been strengthened and consolidated during years of war. We knew we were to attempt the apparently impossible, and there was not a man who did not realize that the shadow of death was crossing the horizon of our lives. Fervently we hoped that the preliminary bombardments had shattered the enemy *morale* and their lines. It did not strike us so forcibly now that the men who were holding the trenches during these final bombardments might have preferred the enemy to be left alone, so that they could be left alone, just like we had wished when we were there.

Personal opinion can always be adapted to the needs of the moment.

A drum-head service was held on the afternoon of the fifth of June, a most unusual occurrence for a weekday, and it was different to all other services I had attended. Shorn of its military glamour, religion found its proper sphere. Men sang hymns with reverence and prayed with understanding. It reached the heart and the soul, and more than one quivering lip was amongst that huge audience.

> Onward Christian Soldiers,
> Marching as to war.

All knew that splendid tune, and the voice of the battalion was the voice of one man.

I seemed to see behind those distant German lines a similar service, with men praying for strength to withstand the shock of attack, with men earnestly singing, perhaps, that very hymn.

> At the sign of triumph
> Satans host doth flee.

And I seemed to hear, after the battle, the people of one country thanking God that he had been with them, and had given them strength to go so far, and the people of the other country thanking God that he had been with them, and had given them strength to stop the enemy from coming any further. So ridiculous, so tragic that Christian men should appeal to God to destroy man, but it was so.

CHAPTER XIV

BATTLE OF THE RIDGES

THE battalion was marching towards the line in platoons at intervals of about one hundred yards. On the side of the road was the divisional band, and as each platoon came within a certain distance the conductor, with a swing, commenced the chorus of "Take me back to dear old Blighty".

It was a stroke of genius. It brought smiles and laughter to the men; perhaps the last real smile, the last real laugh that many would live to enjoy.

We halted on a piece of grassland near the main road, for the day was still young and the sun must go down before we crossed the open road which led to the assembly trenches.

The three other battalions forming the brigade were already spread over the same ground, and there was nothing to screen us from the view of enemy aircraft should they hover near.

Fortunately our superiority in the air at that time was so marked that not a German plane was seen. The sun was shining gloriously and we lay dozing and basking, and thinking of things that were pleasant, or trying not to think of things that were unpleasant.

Shorty lay at my feet chewing a blade of grass, his

thick lips moving vigorously and with evident enjoyment. Mark, with the cheerful air of a proprietor, was looking at the Lewis gun which lay near him comfortably shrouded with a ground-sheet to protect the working parts from dust.

Shorty was getting on in the world. He was a lance-corporal now; not that it made any difference in his attitude to us, or of ours to him, but it had brought a change in the personnel of the gun-team. Mark was number one, and I was to act as his second-in-command. I had reached the revolver stage, and was rather proud of the possession of the "Colt" which I carried in the holster attached to my belt.

Mark opened the conversation.

"The major's servant told me that they are going to explode a mine in front of us," he said.

We pricked up our ears. News from the major's servant was the most reliable that could be obtained.

"Hope they take the blasted thing far enough out," grunted Shorty. He had unhappy recollections of a mine which blew up nearer to our lines than had been intended.

"I shouldn't wonder if the whole darned trench system isn't mined. They've been at it since 1914," I said.

"Yes, it wouldn't surprise me either. I wish to God mines and every darned thing connected with war was in purgatory," added Shorty.

"Funny thing," said Mark, "we can't have above two days' sunshine together but what some stunt's on the go. If it wasn't this job it would be something else as bad."

"They mean yer to earn yer bob a day," Shorty replied. "Hullo! here's the mail."

We made a general rush for the corporal who was carrying the company's letters, and presently I was the happy possessor of three.

"You lucky beggar," said Shorty, "you get half the blinkin' mail."

Shorty always contended that I had more than my fair share of the post. He would totally disregard the fact that if they were not addressed to me there would be so many less in the mail-bag. Sometimes his face would be a study of indignation while the post-corporal read out the names. Usually we had them sorted into platoons and the sum total of correspondence to be issued would not be great. The N.C.O. would shout out my name, then two or three others, and then mine again.

"What, another!" Shorty would exclaim. "You must write lonely soldier letters to all the old maids. What! How many more. Good Lord, give somebody else a chance. I should think so, and about time, too." This, as he finds one addressed to him.

I rather think that the greatest shock Shorty ever received in this life was when he was expecting the arrival of a postal order and was impatiently awaiting the coming of the mail. It came. Five letters, a parcel, and two newspapers, all addressed to me.

Shorty had few correspondents, but we got used to seeing a distinctive envelope with feminine handwriting.

"My cousin," he always told us, and "my cousin" she had to remain, for we never got any nearer the truth.

BATTLE OF THE RIDGES

Evening was drawing near, and preparations were made for a move. We formed up in companies and were loaded with the varied gear which is always carried for an attack. Every alternate man carried a spade, which was thrust down the brace of his equipment at the back. The first platoon moved away towards Vierstraate. Mark shouldered the gun, and I the bag of spare parts, and presently we were marching along the main road. On passing through La Clytte we were somewhat surprised and not a little perturbed to find enemy shells bursting well towards the road, and the further we advanced, the thicker they became. Shells near La Clytte had been unthinkable. We passed fresh gun positions, hundreds of them, each with a handy stack of ammunition, and such stacks, too.

A new direction was taken, and after sundry halts, during one of which I contrived to lose my water through a defective cork, we eventually reached the support line, where we settled down to await the coming of dawn.

Between the supports and the front line a new trench had been dug, and this was crowded with the men who comprised the second wave, the first wave, of course, being in the front line.

The trench which we were occupying was filled with troops, some sprawled on the bottom, others sitting on the firestep. It wanted a couple of hours to the start of the barrage and the waiting period was agonizing. The men were generally cool, or appeared cool. There surely never was a man who could await the commencement of battle without some kind of qualms, and there was never a man who honestly was unafraid of shell-fire when he was exposed to it; and shell-fire we feared more than anything that night, for if the enemy had bombarded the assembly trenches the result would have been appalling.

Happily we suffered no such experience. The guns which had been firing persistently quietened down and there developed an uneasy silence.

"Good Lord," said Mark, "isn't it weird. Why don't they open out."

I looked at my watch and saw that it wanted twenty minutes to three. Zero was at the hour. The very silence awakened those who were dozing, and they began to stretch and yawn and solicit anxious inquiries as to the time, and then——

There was a huge tearing crash, the trench shook as if by an earthquake, and over the length of front from Hill 60 to Messines appeared a scene like so many volcanoes in eruption. Simultaneously, from the rear came the dreadful roar of a thousand cannon, and the rattle of countless machine-guns.

The battle had begun. It was bewildering. The volume of sound made men sweat in an agony of fear. Looking over the parapet we could see nothing but smoke and the flames of exploding shells.

Our turn was not yet. For half an hour the barrage played on the German first system of trenches and then lifted to the second line. Presently, wounded men began to appear, followed by a few Germans, white, haggard, and half-crazy with fright. One big German, naked to the waist, and with horrible wounds on his face, chest, and back, staggered in our direction.

Shorty bawled to him to cross the trench by the

bridge which had been placed near us overnight. The wounded man misunderstood, and thinking that some fresh horror was overtaking him, suddenly gathered strength and took a flying leap into the midst of us. This was rather startling, but with the help of a certain amount of dumb show, we directed him to the nearest dressing-station, and after we had assisted him out of the trench he went his way.

The second line was taken and more wounded and prisoners came into view. Carrying parties with bombs and ammunition set out for the new lines, and then came the order to advance.

We jumped out of the trench, relieved that the long wait was over, and after getting into some sort of order, we marched in artillery formation across the open ground. I felt curiously helpless. The din of the guns behind and the shells in front prevented us from hearing whether the enemy artillery was in action, but no shells appeared to be bursting anywhere near. I fully expected to hear the sudden roar of high explosives, or the crash of shrapnel, but it was singularly absent and we gained confidence with every step. The platoon officer, as fussy as ever, quickly became annoyed because we failed to keep together.

"You'll all get lost," he shrieked. He was like a sheep-dog rounding up the strays, but his efforts were of no avail, for the ground was intersected with shell-holes, which necessitated much breaking apart. We crossed the enemy front line, which was but the wreckage of a trench system, and when nearing the second line we opened into extended order just as we had done in the rehearsals of a few days before.

Still not a hostile shell was noticed, and it became fairly obvious that the German batteries had either been disabled or withdrawn.

We were now on top of the ridge, and glancing back I could see the earthwork of the old British trenches plainly visible. It seemed strange that we had been allowed to live in those obvious targets. Stranger still that these operations had actually commenced without even an attempt to flatten them out. Quite slowly we advanced. Here was a man ablaze with the fire of a dozen Verey lights which had become ignited by some unknown means. He was beyond human aid and his body was left to the mercy of others with more time to investigate.

The second line was garrisoned with khaki-clad soldiers, who were busily engaged deepening and strengthening the trench, and slightly in advance of this position we were required to wait while the barrage reduced our objective, the Black Line.

We crouched in shell-holes watching the vivid scene, and some tried to converse, but their voices were lost in such a terrific clatter. I heard Shorty shout in my ear:

"Where the deuce is Jerry's barrage?" but I shook my head. I wanted to look around.

In a nearby shell-hole sat the commanding officer looking cool and imperturbed, and close to him were various details from the Headquarters unit.

To the right, to the left, and to the immediate front, the barrage, lifting up columns of earth, which was falling in a nerve-broken cascade. I wondered what the enemy was doing in that hell but a few yards away. Lying low, I thought, waiting grimly to meet bayonet with bayonet. I was wrong. We had no fight for the possession of the third line. Even before the barrage had lifted some Germans began to run the gauntlet of the shells, and directly it passed over them they swarmed out of the trench without weapons and with hands extended upwards.

With repeated cries of "*Kamerad*" they rushed towards us, and the extraordinary sight was witnessed of hundreds of British advancing and of hundreds of Germans passing unmolested through their ranks. The Black Line had been entirely evacuated, but it was not now the practice to hold enemy trenches, and we pushed on to some distance in front and there commenced digging. Presently, another regiment came along and leap-frogged through us and dug in a few hundred yards ahead so that we were again in supports. This one-sided battle was now developing in an unexpected manner. Considerably more than the original objective had been taken and apparently the German front on this sector was broken.

Half a dozen tanks came wobbling along and disappeared through a wood which lay half-right from where we had entrenched. A British aeroplane, which had been flying backwards and forwards dangerously near the ground, was hit by a shell and burst into flames, and it was with intense pity that we watched it go to its doom, for the pilot had been a source of inspiration from the commencement.

Our hopes that the attack had ended were dispelled. Towards midday, orders were received to continue the advance, and we again took up the lead and proceeded in the direction taken by the tanks. A road was cut through the wood and we walked warily, but there was no opposition, not even a sniper. Our star was surely in the ascendant this day. On the side of the road was a light railway track, and following it round a bend we encountered several sideless trucks piled high with German dead, iron chains securing them in position. One of the trucks had been struck by a shell and overturned, and the sight was revolting. Reports had been rife about a German grease factory. I know nothing about grease factories, and prefer to believe that the Germans with their usual thoroughness adopted every possible means to remove their dead to the rear for burial in the proper cemeteries.

Through the wood and on to the desolate little hamlet of Oosttaverne, and here we stayed and once more dug ourselves in, and other troops passed through and, encountering machine-gun fire, they crowned the advance by forming a new front line.

The advanced troops were then withdrawn and others took their places. We also retired to the outskirts of the wood and discovered that there had been amazing activity, for several lines of trenches had sprung into existence and were manned with an immense number of troops.

Tired and weary after the long advance, we settled down and awaited the coming of night, and with it the expected counter-attack.

I was glad of the rest, for the bag of spare parts was no featherweight and I knew that Mark, with the gun, was in a similar pickle. I had suffered horribly from thirst and had had good cause to regret the misfortune which had deprived me of my water, but I had somewhat foolishly, and regardless of orders and the diseases which lingered there, drunk from a pool of stagnant water, and this to a certain extent had alleviated the distress which at times threatened to become unbearable.

Enemy shelling, which had recommenced early in the afternoon, was increasing rapidly, and was spread over a wide area, and although it was extremely unlikely that any definite target was being fired on, yet, even so our casualties began to be fairly numerous. One heavy shell exploded near to the trench, killing one man and wounding two others, all belonging to the platoon, and taking this as the forerunner of something worse to follow, we set to with a will, and dug and delved until we were satisfied that we had done all that could be done to ensure safety.

The sun began to settle over the horizon and machine-gun fire from the front line became more apparent. We "stood to" early in readiness for what might come. Suddenly, with a rattle, the whole front blazed with rifle-fire, and from several points rockets sailed majestically into the air to open into pairs of coloured lights, the British signal for artillery for that occasion. Barely had the lights commenced to float above the trenches when the guns from behind were sending a tornado of shells on to the open ground facing the front line. The barrage had commenced with the astonishing promptitude which was only possible through every gun having a shell already in the breech. Lewis guns were mounted on the parapet and every rifle pointed in the direction of the advanced trench, for it was not impossible that the latter would be retaken and our own position assaulted. Apparently, however, the intensive barrage and rifle fire was so destructive that the counter-attack was nipped in the bud.

Then followed a night of intermittent shelling, which at dawn culminated with a protective barrage from the batteries to discourage enemy activity, and the new ground was now definitely won and held.

Quite early the next morning a tall person with red tabs and braided hat came serenely along the new lines. He was the Brigadier-General, and accompanying him was his servant carrying a huge bundle of papers. These the General distributed among the troops, much to their satisfaction, for thoughtfulness of this nature could be appreciated.

Shorty secured a newspaper and settled down at the bottom of the trench, with his back to the one side and his feet pushed well into the earth on the other. Somehow, he was always in trouble with his legs. There was never just enough room for them, and if he stood on them they pushed his head up higher than anyone else, and in shallow trenches this meant that he was required to adopt a perpetual hump-backed attitude for his own safety.

I was struggling with a tin of bully, the flap of which had broken, and I was undecided as to whether I should decapitate it with a bayonet or go round it with a jack-knife, when I was interrupted by Shorty.

"Well, if this ain't the goods," he roared. "Here we are, squatting two or three miles in front of the old line, and according to this we haven't been in it."

A salvo of shells tore shrieking overhead to burst violently a hundred yards behind.

"No, it don't seem like it," said Mark, who had just finished cleaning his revolver and was wiping his fingers on more "four by two" than he was strictly entitled to possess.

"Ulster's day, Canada's day, and I suppose the county regiments will come up in the rations, as per usual," continued Shorty. "Too much bluff, too much soft soap, that's what it is."

"Good propaganda," I suggested.

"That may be," answered Shorty. "But it ain't cricket, all the same. It mentions Wytschaete, that's over there on the right, and Oosttaverne, which is just in front, but they seem to have overlooked that our brigade was the first to get in."

"Better write up about it," said Mark.

"Ah, and I could do that," he replied. "How would this go? The Worcesters, Gloucesters, Staffords, and Warwicks, after carrying everything before them, are now holding on grimly to the new line."

"Eating bully and reading the paper," I added. The newspaper was certainly sounding the praises of the Irish and Colonial regiments; the British units occupying but a modest position in the order of news.

Mark suggested that we should do a little exploring, and as the ground was safely hidden from direct observation, we agreed. Within easy reach lay several dugouts, which we duly inspected. Every indication of a hurried retreat was to be seen. Rifles, with bayonets fixed, stood outside. Equipment was strewn about, and in the dugouts we discovered partially eaten meals. One dugout, which we judged to be that of a General, or some highly placed person, was luxuriously furnished with arm-chairs and couches, and boasted a splendid carpet, which, had it been possible, we should surely have brought back with us. An abundance of bread was found, but we knew better than to sample it for it was extremely probable that poison traps had been laid to catch the unwary.

I unearthed a box of cartridges, made with the bullets reversed so that instead of the pointed end striking the target, the back with the larger surface would do so, thereby causing a much greater wound. I kept one of them as a permanent relic.

The spirit of "souveniring" seized us and we commandeered bayonets, rifle bolts, and many odds and ends, which not long afterwards we were glad to get rid of because of the trouble of carrying them about. Enemy bayonets and other curiosities might look nice at some future happy date, hanging on the wall at home, but to the infantryman, who carries his belongings on his back, every pound of additional weight becomes so much extra burden. I-led off with a collection of six bolts, two bayonets, and a detonated egg bomb, and when finally I landed in England only the egg-bomb remained.

On the third day from the commencement of the battle we were waiting to be relieved at dusk. The German guns had been quiet for fully a couple of hours, but just when we were expecting the incoming troops a distress rocket was fired in the front line, and for hours we "stood to" amid the clamour of the two barrages. Wild rumours were circulated to the effect that the front line had fallen, but happily this proved untrue. When we eventually got away we had the unpleasant experience of being shelled as far back as the old front line.

The guns were in position on the "No Man's Land"

of but a few days ago, and the progress which the engineers had made with roads, light railways, and water-pipes, was remarkable.

How we cheered the gunners when we reached them. Called them jolly good sports. Praised their splendid barrages (which had made our teeth chatter), drank their tea, and carried on contentedly, with cigarettes aglow, to the Ypres-Bailleul road.

Not far from there was our temporary camp, and we settled down to fried bacon, tea, and bread, read letters, felt frightfully important and really happy, and went to sleep.

CHAPTER XV

SOME REFLECTIONS

My first thoughts on awakening from a twelve hours' sleep was of deep gratitude that the thing was over. My second impression was of bitterness. I had passed through one crisis but to prepare for another. The war had only just begun in the sense that victory could only be attained by a succession of battles similar to the one we had just completed. For many days the thoughts of that coming "push" had filled my mind with hopes and fears, and the fear of death had always been predominant. It is strange that mortals who are born to die should quail when they think of the inevitable; yet youth, strong, healthy, vigorous youth, with the fresh wine of life running madly through his veins, sees in death something remote, something which belongs to another sphere, and rightly so, for in the perfect life death is but the peaceful passing of the aged, the gradual running down of the clock of life. Death should never be the perquisite of youth. How pleasant was the thought of the normal life that our fathers and their fathers lived: unhampered by stark raving fear, passing from decade to decade in blissful security and enjoying life and the love of others. God, why cannot the youth of our day live and die like Christians? Why must they exist and suffer worse than the beasts of the field? Hunted and pursued, driven and cajoled. This is not life, it is but a mockery. I wanted to cast off the shackles which bound me. I wanted to breathe the pure air of freedom, to put behind me once and for all those bloody scenes which men call war.

I sat up and looked about me. The inside of the hut had the appearance of an untidy marine stores. Clothes and equipment was scattered about in heaps. Men were lying in all positions snoring, and perhaps dreaming of happier times when shells have ceased to burst and sergeant-majors ceased to roar. They will wake up soon and be happy because the battle is over and they have escaped. Happy because they have been granted a further respite, perhaps for some just a few days' grace at the most. And there is not an old face amongst them, not a man above twenty-five, mere boys. Surely youth is paying the price; youth is the sacrifice that age may live on and fulfil its destiny.

My thoughts reverted to the battle. It had been an extraordinary affair. We had not fired a shot with the gun, for the simple reason that we had not once been presented with a target, and we had returned stronger in numbers than we had dared to hope. Men had died, as men must always die under such conditions; but, generally speaking, we had been fortunate. In other sectors regiments had not advanced so far and had fared much worse. Certain conceptions of mine had been radically altered. All Germans were not square-headed monstrosities. I had seen intelligent-looking men, who in their rightful spheres might have been schoolmasters, or professors of ethics, or anything which embodied the finer points of life.

They were unkempt and to some extent wild in appearance, but they had endured sufficient of hell to make them. I know that I had experienced a feeling akin to sympathy. They were not in the war of their own free will. They could not keep out if they had wished to. They possessed families, and lived in homes infinitely more comfortable than the best dugout on the Messines ridge.

That they were out to kill was certain, but, like us, they must kill to save themselves. War is the supreme despoiler of human nature and human ideals. Life is so abominably cheap. There are no inquests, no inquiries. If you get killed, you might get buried pretty smartly, or you might be left to rot where you fall. No one worries. There are plenty more being fattened in the camps at home. What does it matter if one man dies, or a dozen, or a thousand. That piece of trench may be of little military value, but if G.H.Q. wants it they will have it even at the price of a dead man to a square foot. Why worry. "Killed in action" covers a multitude of sinners, and incompetence is adequately covered by a pensions department. War and peace offer parallel absurdities. In normal times a regiment of men would be ordered to break up a monument if it would save the life of a man pinned underneath. In times of war a trench or hillock must be saved if it costs the lives of a regiment to do it.

During war a man can go out on patrol and creep up behind one of his opponents whom he has never previously seen, and to whom he bears no personal malice, and he can split his skull and receive the plaudits of his superiors, with perhaps a medal in addition, and the wife of the man with the split skull will receive notification that her husband had died fighting, and a weekly dole, and nothing more need be said.

In peace time, a man who splits the skull of another man, even though in actual fight, gets hung or suffers a long term of imprisonment, and the dividing line between the two deeds is exceedingly small.

Comparatively few men die fighting in modern warfare. The phrase is extensively used, but most men die without the chance of a fight, without a glimpse of the slayer. A soldier crouching at the bottom of a trench which is blown up is not fighting, in the true sense of the word. He is taking cover, just as a civilian takes cover during a bombing raid. A man making a road three miles behind the line is not fighting when shrapnel claims him as a victim. He is under fire, certainly, but the difference between being under fire and fighting is the difference between the modern war and the old.

Fighting is an elastic term which allows for a great deal of expansion. Modern warfare is legalized murder, nothing less, and modern warfare, because of its very intensity and consumption of man-power, has made the peoples of all nations the slaves of the war-lords.

CHAPTER XVI

HOLDING AN ADVANCED LINE

THE day following our return from the battle of the ridges we were under canvas in a position a little to the left of Kemmel, and just at the edge of the camp was the arm of a broad-gauge railway. Periodically, an engine drawing a twelve-inch gun would pull into the arm and a few rounds would be fired, after which the engine would steam away. It caused something of a commotion when we first heard it.

We had been discussing the good fortune of a fellow who had been sent home to work on munitions, and Shorty was lamenting the fact that he was unable to follow such a pleasant example.

"He'll have his nights and his week-ends, pounds in his pocket, plenty of grub, and no more stinkin' trenches to worry about," he murmured, with a melancholy air. "Lucky dog, if ever there was one."

"Why, Shorty, you don't want your ticket, do you?" said Mark, winking at me.

"Don't want it. I like that bit. Give me the chance and half-hour's start, and you won't see my boots for dust. D'ye know what I'd do willingly for my ticket?"

He looked round expectantly.

"What's that?" we asked.

"I'd crawl to Bolon on my hands and knees."

"So would I," Mark answered, and I agreed also.

"And there ain't a chap here who wouldn't do the same," continued Shorty, glaring round the tent.

Shorty's line of argument was evidently acceptable if the wild declarations of some of the fellows could be relied upon. One thought that his left arm would be a fair price to pay for his discharge. Another would not object to losing a couple of fingers for a like reward. As the latter said:

"I should have some left and be sure of them, but as things are I'm not certain that I shall finish up with the need for fingers."

"What say you, Cherub?" asked Shorty.

The fellow he addressed was the latest recruit to the gun-team and had only lately come to the battalion from the training camp. He was only a boy, a little over nineteen years of age, but looked younger, with a round pleasing face, fresh-coloured and good-looking. He would have been better served sitting in the parish church with cassock and surplice, but here he was, in the war and the trenches.

He was far from being a milksop, for he could march with the best, show coolness under fire, and look after himself generally. It was his innocent expression that earned for him the title of the Cherub.

Before he had the opportunity of replying to Shorty's query there was a terrific crash which shook the camp.

"What the hell!" exclaimed Shorty.

We all darted outside and found the big gun in position. That immediately commenced another discussion as to why they should want to bring the darned thing here, as if we didn't hear enough of them up yonder, and if they had got to bring it here why couldn't they move us somewhere else and give chaps a chance.

That gun got on our nerves. It was always going off at the least-expected times. It would creep up in the middle of the night and arouse the camp. It had a nasty habit of firing just as you were near enough for the wind to blow your hat off.

We never could settle down to it, but it did not worry us for long, because in a few days we were making tracks across country to relieve the advanced positions. Getting there was an arduous task, for it was not impossible to walk into the German line by mistake. One battalion had already lost a gun-team in this manner. Their guide had led them into what he thought was the proper position, but it was the wrong side of some German outposts, and they were bagged as neatly as possible. We had the curious experience of hearing the familiar tap-tap of the Lewis coming from their lines.

The front line was not a complete trench as we understood it. It consisted of a series of holes hurriedly dug during the advance. Some attempt had been made to link them up, but the connections were not nearly the proper depth to afford protection.

The gun-team was accommodated in a piece of trench which possessed two traverses, forming something like the letter Z. On the right was the partly-dug communication, which led to company headquarters about fifty yards away, and on the left, the ground was untouched, but the right wing of another regiment was within easy distance. The outgoing unit told us to expect heavy shelling, and we got it. They strafed us so violently that the guns were signalled for retaliation. The next day was much the same. Quite early in the morning heavy shrapnel commenced bursting overhead and uncommonly close to the ground. Then high explosives began to be mixed with them. After an hour of near squeaks a shell exploded at the back of the traverse, almost smothering us in earth and dust. We heard a cry from the next traverse, and Mark and I groped round the bend. It was hardly possible to see a yard in front because of the smoke, and the fumes made us choke and gasp.

A man was lying in the trench, groaning pitifully. It was the Cherub. We raised him off the ground and saw that he was terribly wounded in the back. I cut away his equipment and clothes while Mark produced a field dressing. It was scarcely big enough to cover the wound.

The Cherub looked at us with sorrowful eyes. "He's trying to say something," said Mark. I bent down, but could distinguish only one word, "Mother."

I felt wildly impatient and decided to crawl for assistance to company headquarters. This I accomplished safely, and returned with a stretcher-bearer who made a better job of the dressing.

The Cherub was mortally wounded and with every breath the blood gushed from the hole in his back. He wanted to lie down on the bottom of the trench. His hands moved expressively as though he wished us to understand something that his lips could not express. The shells were still bursting near and I could have cried out in agony for a few minutes' truce while the boy was got safely away.

We hoisted him upon the back of the stretcher-bearer, who was indeed a brave man, and he carried him away along that half-dug trench.

Later, we heard with infinite sorrow that our poor Cherub had died on the way to the dressing-station. Emblem of the flower of the youth of England, your passing has multiplied the bitterness that is within us.

The weather became decidedly hot and the acrid shell fumes engendered a thirst which was impossible to satisfy, with the limited amount of water at our disposal. The rations and water were brought up nightly, and distributed immediately after "stand-down" in the morning. It is surprising how hungry a man can become when exposed to the air indefinitely. We were always hungry, and if the rations had been trebled we should never have had too much.

On the third morning we were impatiently waiting for Shorty to begin the usual share-out. One man was engaged looking through the periscope, and the remainder were lolling about casting ravenous eyes on the sandbag which contained the provisions for the ensuing twenty-four hours.

"Two loaves," said Shorty.

That was a quarter of a loaf for each, a pound of bread if it was full weight, but the loaves looked small, and a housewife in England would have been keenly suspicious if she had been offered one as a two-pound loaf.

Three tins of pork-and-beans, one with the top bulging unhealthily, one bully, one Maconochie, and a tin of milk, a few biscuits, a small piece of cold fat bacon, and a ragged lump of boiled beef with tea, and sugar and sandbag hairs liberally adhering to it.

"Perish those cooks," said Shorty. "They haven't tied the tea up properly."

The bottom corners of the sandbag always held the tea and sugar, and pieces of string tied securely were usually sufficient to keep it in its place, but on this occasion the corners had either not been fastened properly or the bag had been roughly handled. In any case, the tea and sugar had worked loose and so got on the meat.

It was always annoying to find that the food had been mishandled, and there were times when we had just cause for complaint. In extremely bad weather, when the ration party has been obliged to make use of water-logged trenches, the bags have literally been dragged through mud and water, with the consequence that the bread has been a pulp and we have had to eat it or go without.

The division took place and the rations were voted "not so bad". It required a certain amount of tact to satisfy everyone. The solitary tin of Maconochie was the chief anxiety. We all liked it, and finally the tin was opened and passed round, and each man took a share as marked by Shorty's jack-knife.

The can of water was next produced and water-bottles or mess-tins were quickly forthcoming, and as each man received his portion he retired to his corner to do justice to it. "Tommy's Cookers" came on the scene. Originally, these were prepared tins of solidified methylated spirit which burned without smoke, and were distinctly useful, for it was possible even in the most advanced position to enjoy hot tea with their assistance. Our battalion had gone one worse and made their own with a combination of sawdust and petrol, and they were not nearly so efficient.

Mark smelled his share of water and looked at Shorty. Shorty had a sniff and looked at me. I picked up my mess-tin and smelt petrol.

"Somebody should swing for this," said Shorty.

One of the men put a light to his share. It began to blaze furiously but was quickly thrown on the bottom of the trench and the flames stamped out. What had happened was that by some mistake a tin containing so much petrol had been filled with water and sent up as usual.

Another day of torrid heat and we should be parched. We cursed those cooks with full-blooded English expletives, and as the day progressed and it became hotter, with the full heat of a midsummer sun, we became excessively thirsty, more so because there was nothing to drink. On the afternoon, heavy clouds came over and a thunderstorm broke. Mess-tins were opened. Ground-sheets, which would have kept the wet out, were held bag fashion to keep the wet in. It rained in torrents. It thundered, and lightning stabbed the sky with vivid flashes. Water began to trickle into the trench, and to make matters worse the shelling recommenced. In ten minutes we had more water than we required, and it was still coming. In half an hour it was pouring over the parapet and we were standing knee-deep. Never did mortal man have his prayers answered more readily, and when the rain had ceased and we found the "Tommy's Cookers" so saturated that they were useless, we began to realize that the cure was worse than the complaint.

Getting away from that post was something of an ordeal, for the Germans were shelling the tracks to the rear, and the platoon officer was not over-confident of keeping to the proper direction. We followed him for about half a mile and then he declared he was lost. Five-point-nines were crashing with uncomfortable monotony, and the impatience of the men only served to increase his distress.

"We shall damn well get killed hanging about here," yelled one man with obvious lack of restraint.

"Move on, sir, let's get out of this."

But the officer was in a quandary. There was not much moonlight, and there was a long way to go, and to take the wrong direction would bring forth a storm of criticism that a dozen boxes of "Woodbines" would not allay. Fortunately, the man from Walsall, who never cleaned out the little hole in his rifle, volunteered to act as guide, an offer which the officer promptly accepted, and the said man from Walsall with astonishing celerity led us back to the guns.

These night reliefs from warm corners of the line were always fraught with anxiety for those who took part in them. The keenness of the men to get away would be emphasized from the start, and the pace, which was invariably hot, became hotter past known danger points. Men would look back to see how far they were putting the trenches behind, and instinctively shudder when they realized that they had still to pass the spot where so and so got killed coming in.

No matter what little sleep the troops had had, or

what they had been forced to endure, they always seemed to have stored sufficient reserve energy to assist them on the homeward track. I had by now become used to these furious bursts of speed and could keep abreast of the others without undue strain. So they would continue until the main transport road was reached, and this would often be so crowded as to make progress very slow indeed. Motor-lorries and limbers, reliefs going in, the relieved coming out, working parties, Royal Engineers, ambulances, and remnants of all regiments jostling each other in the dark like a crowd in a busy street at home. Generally an hour's walk from the front line would bring one out of the direct danger zone, and then it was possible to rest and smoke and smile to yourself, realizing that, at least, a few days of glorious life were assured.

CHAPTER XVII

A NIGHT OF TERROR

TOWARDS the end of June, the battalion moved into the old front line, and for over a month this served as our reserve quarters from the fighting line. We held most of the usual out-of-the-line parades, with the accompanying orgy of cleaning-up and being inspected, and as we lived and slept in just an ordinary trench, it was a case of being half-in and half-out of the line.

Shorty, Mark, and myself occupied a tiny little shelter in the side of the trench, just big enough for the three of us to lie down comfortably. We called it home, and it was home to us, for we contrived to make ourselves as comfortable as one could wish under such circumstances. From it we sallied forth to do the customary spells in the advanced positions, and to its hospitable shelter we returned, tired and weary, but glad of a "home" to come back to.

During one of these spells in the line the gunners were living in the usual hope of an early relief. We had come back into the supports and had taken temporary charge of a concrete "pill-box", of which many were dotted about these sectors. I had just been telling Shorty of the enjoyable time we would have when we got back "home", for I was expecting a couple of well-filled parcels, and Shorty, who could always enjoy a share of anyone's parcel, was waxing eloquent and hoped that there would be tinned pears with cream to suit.

"I like pears and cream," he said, licking his lips,

At this juncture the platoon officer appeared at the entrance to the "pill-box". The look on his face denoted something unpleasant, and he immediately commenced to unburden his mind.

"The company is doing a stunt to-night," he said, drawing a trench map from his pocket. He opened it and pointed with his pencil.

"We leave the trench at this point and creep to the rear of the tree stumps, that you have seen from the front line. That first building in front of the trees is unoccupied and we shall take no notice of it. We shall carry on until we come to this point, Junction Buildings. We might get some opposition there, but it won't be much because they are going to trench-mortar it. I am told that it is a farmhouse which has been converted into a stronghold, and when we have taken that place we shall entrench and link up with the present front line. That is all."

"Humph," grunted Shorty. "It sounds all right, but it will spoil our party, sir; someone is expecting a feed down at the back and we were in it till this cropped up."

"Oh, that can wait until we get back," said the officer pleasantly. "Now all be ready to proceed to the front line in an hour's time." He crawled away and left us gasping.

"What the blazes do they take us for. No other

blinkin' battalion gets put on like curs does," said Shorty.

"Damn the trench-mortars, they do more harm than good on a job like this," I put in.

"That's talking about being relieved," continued Shorty. "Some of you chaps expect to be relieved before you get here."

"Just hark at him, the one who likes pears with cream," said Mark.

Shorty treated the remark with studied indifference.

"I don't care about the trench-mortar side of the business," he said. "It's just about as good as a knock on the door to say we're coming. They'd oughter plaster it with heavies. If they knocked the infernal thing down, it wouldn't want any taking."

Mark chewed the end of his cigarette reflectively.

"It strikes me there's more in it than they bargain for," said he. "Just walk round here and dig in there; sounds like a kid's game, but is it?"

"You'll see what's in it when the trench-mortars get going. Up will go his lights and down will come his barrage, and if we aren't well up to the front the stunt will finish at the start," concluded Shorty.

It was natural to grouse. No one would care to continually risk their lives without a grumble, and soldiers are no exception to the rule.

The next hour was spent in preparation, overhauling the gun, cleaning magazines and rifles, and then the head of the platoon officer again appeared in the doorway, and without more ado we went along the trench to the front line.

It would be about eleven o'clock at night when we crept into "No Man's Land", and through the barbed wire on this unwholesome task. In the meantime, we had viewed Junction Buildings, and it certainly had a lamb-like appearance, from the distance. The moon was obscured by a cloud and consequently there was little danger of being seen. It would have been quite possible to creep unobserved right up to the building, but our instruction was to wait by the tree stumps for the trench-mortar strafe. It commenced with three bombs which dropped short, and the attacking party scattered. This was a bad start, for a stampede on a dark night when men are armed with rifles and bayonets is a dangerous procedure, but happily no one was hurt and the next shots were lifted to a point nearer the objective. As we had foreseen, the enemy, alarmed by the bursting of these huge bombs, immediately fired his appeal for artillery support, and we knew then that the safest course to pursue was to advance out of reach of the barrage which could be expected any second. We advanced to within fifty or sixty yards of the building, and none too soon, for the enemy shells came crashing on the ground between the tree stumps and the front line.

As ill-luck would have it, the moon came from behind the cloud and illuminated the scene for the benefit of the German garrison, who until then had no idea that an attack was actually in progress, and at once a hail of rifle and machine-gun bullets swept the ground. At least one officer and a dozen men were immediately casualties and the advance was checked. Some of the men began to retreat, but Shorty, his huge bulk clearly visible, brought them to a standstill by threatening to turn the gun on them.

The troops then lay on the ground and fired at the loopholes of the building, but it was a waste of ammunition, for there was not the slightest hope of hitting any of the defenders. For some time we lay there hardly knowing what to do, and we might easily have stayed there the greater part of the night had not the senior sergeant, who was acting-sergeant-major for the occasion, given a shout of "Come on, boys," and this order, galvanizing everyone into action, the whole line charged headlong at the building.

It was a desperately foolish move, for the lamblike building proved to be a concreted fort, and from its vitals poured forth a devastating torrent of bombs and bullets. Many men fell dead, among the first being the acting-sergeant-major, and the company, thoroughly demoralized, fell back to the position they had charged from. Wounded were crawling about in all directions, and in a shell-hole I found the company officer badly wounded and apparently blind, pleading with infinite pathos. "Please take me away from here, someone." Ernie, the one-time guide, was in a similar plight as the result of a bomb, for with sightless eyes and arms outstretched he was endeavouring to seek the way to our original line. Both he and the captain were safely removed during the next few minutes.

Meanwhile, the remainder of the company were utterly at a loss. No officer was left and no one seemed capable of reorganizing the men who were scattered in shell-holes over a fairly wide area. Retreat on the front line was out of the question without definite orders to that effect; for our instructions were to dig a new trench, and something would have to be done towards carrying out those instructions. It was decided to dig in where we lay, and with the starting of a few men the others rapidly followed suit. We knew perfectly well that the position was hopeless, for we were being enfiladed and bombed unmercifully. Rifle grenades and egg-bombs were the biggest source of trouble, but as we gradually got below ground the danger from these was minimized to some extent.

At length we had a trench deep enough to offer sanctuary, and we again took up the task of firing at the loopholes, or at any flash of light which suggested the discharging of a rifle.

The prospect which naturally troubled us was what would happen when daylight came, and our newly dug trench was in full view of the enemy. We knew quite well that their guns would soon get the range and make short work of blowing us out, and we also knew that once the night had gone we should be cut off from the main line without food or water and be forced to crouch there until it again became dark, and fresh instructions reached us.

The hours went slowly by and the first streaks of dawn had begun to shed an eerie light on the scene, when a figure was observed to be creeping from the front line to our advanced position. He reached the extreme right of the company, and immediately the word came along to fall back on the front line. Then ensued a mad stampede for safety.

"One at a time, one at a time," cried a sergeant in my bit of trench, but he was climbing out and I quickly followed his example.

The Germans could now see what was taking place and a fierce volume of fire poured from the building and the adjacent line. Bullets whizzed past me, as bending low, I ran with a small group of others who in their flight had the common sense to run in a zig-zag fashion to lessen the targets which they offered. Here and there a man fell with a bullet in him, but the majority of us reached the barbed wire. It had been cut in one particular place, and the first man got entangled and caused a jam, but fortunately the tree stumps partially obscured the enemy's view, and after much tugging and swearing the path was cleared, and with a last desperate rush we reached the trench and tumbled headlong in.

The front line seemed to me just the safest place in the world. It became a trifle overcrowded because it already held its usual quota of defenders, but nevertheless we stayed there until night, when we were relieved by another regiment. Then we proceeded back to our "home" in reserve, and home it was that night, for hot food was awaiting us, the post had arrived, and with it the expected parcels, which we decided to leave over for the next day, and tired in body, but relieved in mind, I went to sleep with a certain thankfulness in my heart, and the *Weekly Dispatch* over my head.

"D" Company had suffered grievous casualties. Every officer who took part had been wounded, including Lieutenant Drew, the platoon officer. He had maintained his eccentricity to the last. Stretcher-bearers wanted to carry him, but he wanted to walk. Then he would desire to be carried a little and soon afterwards rather walk again; and, finally, he was safely taken away. Perhaps the circumstances of his injury had much to do with the state of indecision, for he was wounded in that portion of the anatomy which allows for sitting down. We had laughed at his traits but we had respected him as an officer and a gentleman, and we felt his loss keenly. Even the man from Walsall was affected, for he had always held for him more than a sneaking regard.

A tragedy was enacted the night that we were relieved. Several men who would not risk the dash for life in the early morning had remained concealed in the newly dug trench by Junction Buildings, until they deemed it advisable to return. When approaching our lines, they were unfortunately shot down in mistake for a raiding party. It is quite obvious that the man who is holding the advanced line carries his life in his hand, and hesitation so often spells death to himself that he dare not take the slightest risk. Had they made the attempt before the line had been taken over by a fresh unit their chances of success would have been immeasurably greater.

A few days later the concrete fort was bombarded with heavies and duly captured, and some of us went to see the prisoners as they were led to the rear. There were twenty-four of them, and more insignificant specimens of soldiers could hardly be imagined. They seemed horribly afraid lest their resistance would ensure some severe punishment, but they had little to worry about, for they were now infinitely safer than we were.

While still occupying our dugout home we had a man sent to us who was the poorest soldier I ever met. He should never have been allowed to leave England, never mind reach the trenches, for he was a bundle of nerves, almost afraid of his own shadow, and quickly became the butt of the most boisterous men in the company. He especially feared Mills bombs and would not touch one unless he was forced to do so. I don't believe he ever learnt to detonate one, for the sight of a "Mills" in the hands of another man was sufficient to start him backing to a safe distance.

One afternoon we were due on a working party at a stated time, and the road that we should have to take was being subjected to much shell-fire. This alarmed us considerably, and almost terrified the nervous one, and when, in full sight of all of us, a shell burst by a limber—killing a mule which the driver quickly released and left behind—the man was in a state of abject terror.

The time came for the working party to set off, and as we reached the danger zone the shelling moderated to such an extent that we had a comparatively easy journey, and the task was completed without a casualty. Upon returning to the trench, however, we learnt with surprise and, I may add, very great sorrow, that the man who was frightened of Mills bombs had shirked the working party, and in the safety of that trench he had kicked a rusty "Mills" which was lying there, and had died of wounds.

We were getting fed-up with this constant in and out of the trenches. For nearly a month we had been living like rats in holes, and we longed for a spell away from the line. There was little or no amusement to be obtained. A concert party gave a show on one occasion, but that only served to whet our appetites for some civilization. Shorty wanted to see some real "wimmen" again. Mark felt that he would like eggs and chips every night for a whole week, and I wished for nothing better than the doubtful comforts of a village barn with plenty of clean straw to lie upon.

It was after "lights out" and we were officially in bed, which meant lying down on a boarded floor, with overcoats for a covering, no blankets being allowed during the summer months. Our little "home" was sufficiently secluded to be away from the observation of any officer or senior N.C.O., and the stump of a candle was burning on its pedestal of tin stuck in the side of the shelter.

Shorty, with the end of a cigarette between his thick lips and his head resting on his pack, was in a pessimistic mood, a very rare occurrence for him.

"This blarsted war will go on for ever," he said. "We shall stick here, day in and day out, until we're too old to fight and then they'll push us in the Labour Corps."

"Cheer up, Shorty, the first seven years are the worst," said Mark.

"It's a war of liberty, isn't it?" I murmured, thinking of the glorious liberty we were enjoying just then."

"Where's the liberty?" growled Shorty.

"*Après la guerre,*" I answered.

"That's too far off to interest me," answered Shorty. "I want some now. If I was to get up and walk fifty yards, some guy would want to know where I was going, and if I stay here after six o'clock in the morning, some guy will want to know when I'm coming. I'm on a piece of string, pulled here and there, and up and down, and where the devil they like."

"That's just how it is," said Mark. "If you wanted

to capture a trench by yourself, you couldn't unless you were told to."

"I don't want to, thanks, unless it's a celery trench," grinned Shorty.

"The trouble is," I remarked, "we are getting more war than we bargained for, and we are all in the same boat. We go into those filthy trenches to be shelled and bombed, and Jerry goes into his trenches and gets the same, and yet the people who started the war or had the most to do with it can live their normal lives in perfect safety."

"It was always like that," said Mark. "In days gone by the wicked old baron used to hire his men to do the dirty work of fighting, and we ourselves are no more than hirelings paid a bob a day to rot in these holes until the big bugs can come to terms. Of course, we all know the parrot cry of King and country, and patriotism, but if a tight fist was kept on the war-mongers it wouldn't be necessary to raise the cry at all."

"What we want to do when the war's over is to vote for the party that believes in peace," put in Shorty, who was evidently becoming inspired.

"That's the idea," I answered. "Put the brake on before anything's doing. It's too late when the ultimatums are flying about. It stands to reason that the chaps with any blood in them at all will come forward like they've always done, when the flag-wagging starts."

"Pity the war-mongers can't have a dose of it," said Mark.

"The whole damn lot ought to be shoved in the front line to fight it out themselves," exclaimed

Shorty. "The war would be over this time to-morrow if half a dozen of each side could taste a barrage to themselves."

"That's the stuff to give 'em," said Mark. "They don't realize the sufferings of the chaps out here, and the way the papers bang the chat makes things worse. Sort of a joy-ride, according to some of the pictures, with 'Tommy all smiles, Tommy likes fighting, and Tommy wants to get at him' sort of bluff."

"You won't see any pictures of the ground round Junction Buildings, before and after," I ventured.

"No fear, they prefer to show the bright spots," Mark continued. "Look at the people who are brought over here on a sort of conducted tour. They are taken round the cushiest parts of the line and they see a shell burst and some war graves, and then go back and write up their experiences in the trenches. Anyone would think by reading some of the accounts that there was a miniature 'Ritz' in every trench. Why don't they take them round the hell spots and let people know the truth?"

The candle was guttering and with a tremendous blow from two yards' range Shorty blew it out and we settled down in the darkness.

The conversation had interested me, for it presented an argument which was indisputable. Why should things be so? Why should not the nations of the world work for the good of each other, and not with the desire to murder and loot and turn the fair places of the world into places of horror? Why should one man be allowed to domineer to such an extent that he could become a menace to the safety of countless millions? Why should I be compelled to stand in ghastly trenches waiting for the end, which was always so near? I had no hatred for any particular man. I never knew a German personally. I knew that they were a thrifty race, musical, artistic, and clever. I knew that they had committed atrocities of an almost unbelievable character, but could we condemn a whole nation for deeds which might be the work of a maddened individual, or which might be committed under the orders of a fanatical General? After all, the masses are but pawns in the game, moved hither and thither by the great masters, or tyrants, whichever word is the most fitting, and pawns we must continue to be until the masses are moved by the greater powers of common sense and common justice, and have the courage to cry "checkmate."

CHAPTER XVIII

TROUBLE IN THE FRONT LINE

ABOUT the end of the third week in July we went into support with the idea of doing twenty-four hours and then getting relieved by another division, after which, it was said, we should go back for the long-expected rest. The twenty-four hours was increased to four days, and, at the expiration of that time, we found that we were under orders for a spell in the front line.

We had experienced a fairly easy time until then, but directly we set foot in a communication trench on the first stage of the journey, the trouble commenced.

Different parts of the trench were successively bombarded with heavies, and these kept us running backwards and forwards as the various portions were covered by the strafe. The trench ran a considerable distance and then came to a dead end, and the remaining part of the journey was over the open ground. It was an uncanny experience. The night was dark and there were ghostly bits of woods to traverse, with here and there the remnant of a building, desolate and uninviting. The creak of a swaying rafter or the snapping of a broken twig would jar the nerves, and spur each one to keep close contact with the other. The contour of the front was outlined with the brilliant star-shells of the enemy and the bark of a machine-gun denoted that we were approaching the advanced trench.

The business of taking-over was but the matter of a few seconds, and we immediately began to make ourselves comfortable by scooping out small holes which would permit a sitting posture. The trench was shallow and there was no firestep, but we could see all that we wished to see by simply standing and looking over.

Shorty had, as usual, inflicted his presence on us, although he was no longer responsible for the gun. His job was divided into keeping a fatherly eye on each of the four guns belonging to the company, but he invariably spent the greater part of his time with us, and if a trench happened to be divided so that the various guns were isolated during daylight, Shorty always found that our position was the most congenial.

Towards midnight I was dozing in a corner of the traverse. Shorty was looking over the top moodily contemplating the lights, and Mark was leaning against the back of the trench puffing a cigarette. Heavy shrapnel burst overhead, and almost immediately I heard Mark groan and saw his body beginning to sag. Shorty and I grabbed him before he could fall and, after investigation, discovered that he was wounded in the stomach. Stretcher-bearers were quickly on the scene, and with a hurried farewell this staunch pal of many months was carried away, and we saw him no more. Weeks later, we heard that he was progressing well but was unlikely to again return to the fighting line.

The loss of Mark was something of a shock, for he had equally shared with us the discomforts and dangers of the trenches, and for a time we felt strangely out of gear. His passing brought me into the first position on the gun-team, and with it I found an additional responsibility which was not altogether unpleasant.

While occupying this trench, we encountered a shell the like of which we had not hitherto experienced. Usually by the sound it makes it is fairly easy to tell whether a shell is going to drop near, or pass well overhead; but this particular shell was the exception to the rule. It gave a peculiar humming noise and was apparently going well behind the lines, but suddenly its speed would seem to increase, and it would burst near the parapet in a most disconcerting manner. It certainly gave us something of a fright, and the only explanation I had offered me when we returned from the line was that in all probability the gun was firing at extreme range. Still, we did not know that much just at the time, and we accepted it as a fresh burst of frightfulness, and the more we heard of the crafty shell the more we wished we could get away from it. A further source of trouble was the heat. It was oppressive. The trench seemed deficient of air and the meat became maggoty, while an intolerable thirst was ever-present.

The shelling on both sides was continuous, and we suspected that the ground was being prepared for another attack. On the night after Mark was wounded it quietened down, and I determined to take advantage of the occasion to get a little sleep. Then, with an overwhelming crash, the Germans placed a barrage on the trench. We were on our feet instantly and Shorty unceremoniously commandeered the gun. An attack was practically certain when the barrage ceased, and we hastily prepared bombs for rapid throwing.

Shorty, in accordance with his usual practice, began talking to the gun which he had pulled off the parapet. I could hear him telling it not to stop firing until it was told to, and to fire straight. His eyes were gleaming with excitement, but his great hands were steady. Shorty had forgotten all about liberty in the stress of the moment. A familiar irritation of the nose indicated that mustard gas-shells were bursting near, so we donned our respirators and awaited events. For fully an hour the barrage continued and then began to die away. We could hear shouts and cries somewhere on the far right, but even the repeated discharge of Verey lights in that direction failed to reveal the least sign of an attack. But an attack had been made, on the unit which linked up with ours, and for a few hours the enemy actually occupied part of the trench, and were only evicted after a fierce struggle. The barrage had been extended to our portion of the line to discourage us from taking a hand in the matter.

For four days we endured all the hell, the misery, and the anxiety that a front line can offer. We were bombed and shelled alternately. Thunderstorms occurred which soaked us through and through. The trench became a quagmire, but the end of the fourth day saw us confidently waiting for the relief which had been expected almost nightly. This was no idle rumour, for the guides had gone forth to bring in the new-comers. It gradually became dark and every minute we were hoping to see the first files of the relief make their appearance, when, to our chagrin and amazement, the distress signal was fired near our own company headquarters. In quick response the British batteries covering the sector opened with a roar and a curtain of fire descended in No Man's Land. We were at a loss to understand the cause of the bother, but found out later that some unduly nervous N.C.O. had seen suspicious movements near the barbed wire.

We cursed with rage to think that a fairly quiet night had been turned into an inferno, for we knew from bitter experience that the enemy would respond to the challenge, and that for hours the roads to the rear would be systematically shelled.

The relief arrived a couple of hours late and, it now being my duty to hand over the gun position, I was soon the only member of the company left in the trench. It became crowded with new-comers, all anxious to find their proper stations so that they could settle down and rest after the fatiguing journey. At this point the peculiar dropping shell made its appearance and caused a commotion amongst the relief.

"Gawd strike, I thought that was going right over," said the man who was taking over the gun position.

Then came another, and soon a perfect torrent of the mysterious shells were bursting near the trench.

"What the hell do they call them, chummy?" asked the man, but I was going and did not wait to discuss the matter. The trench was blocked and I could make no headway beyond the first traverse.

The only alternative was to climb out, which I did, and then without a moment's loss of time I ran for the communication trench. It was further than I had anticipated, and I was glad to rest by a ruined building while I recovered my breath and located the position. Much travelling in and out of the trenches had increased my efficiency in this respect, and I had discarded the helplessness which had been my lot on the Somme.

A shell near the building convinced me that the locality was, not healthy, so I decided to move, and almost before I expected it I struck the trench and, slipping in, made a rapid journey to the other end.

Here I found a great crowd of details from various regiments. The Germans were shelling the road which must be traversed, and the men were going out a few at a time and making a run for it. We queued along the trench like people going into a theatre, and when the road came into view I could see that it was dotted with the bodies of men who had been hit. At first, I decided that the safest plan would be to stay in the trench, but even as the thought entered my mind a deluge of shells exploded on both sides, and I became wildly impatient to reach the head of the queue. From what I could gather, not more than a couple of hundred yards of the road was being shelled, but several shells were dropping each minute and the risk of being hit was very great. The men would wait until one lot of shells had burst and then race like mad to get clear of the danger zone before the next salvo arrived. The party immediately in front of me got away and had almost reached the end of the zone, when a shell burst directly behind them and one of them fell, and stayed there.

The night was clear and visibility was possible for quite a long distance. The crashing of that shell was the signal that it was my turn, and with the spare parts bag over my shoulder (Shorty had taken the gun) I sprinted along the road. Two more men ran alongside me, and we had barely covered half the distance when I heard the oncoming shells shrieking towards us, and knowing by the sound they made that I should be hit, I flung myself on the ground and buried my face in the mud. The explosion partly lifted me off the ground, but I was unhurt and on my feet in a second. The other two were lying a few yards away. I shouted, but received no response, and without waiting for further disaster I ran like one possessed.

The distance that a man will cover when shells are urging him on is remarkable, and although I was heavily burdened, I must have covered half a mile before I slackened speed, and the only reason why I pulled up then was because another part of the road was being subjected to a similar strafe. I was in no mood to risk a second race and I looked for a convenient dugout where I could pass the remainder of the night. There was not the slightest need to attempt to find the company immediately, and I should have a far better chance of locating them during daylight. Coming away from the line was a vastly different proposition to going in. Then a man must keep touch with his unit and must reach the trenches however tired and weary he may become. Men are waiting to be relieved and no excuse other than that of being wounded *en route* would be sufficient to justify one's absence when the relief took place.

A pill-box afforded the protection I desired, and I

crawled through the narrow opening. No ray of light penetrated into that dismal abode, and after I had bruised my shin on something hard I felt for my matches, but discovered I had used them all. I badly wanted a smoke, but there was no hope of one. It would be of no earthly use standing outside waiting for someone to come along, for I had not met a soul since I had left the trench. The next best thing to do was to fashion some kind of a bed, and this I did, and being thoroughly tired, soon fell fast asleep. Once I was awakened by a terrific crash which shook the structure. I guessed it was a direct hit, but I had faith in the German pill-boxes, and I told myself that it was a lucky hit which would not occur again that night.

It was daylight when I awoke, and the light from the entrance showed me that I was surrounded with boxes of all sizes. I had dropped into a bomb store. The sun was shining brilliantly when I crept out of my temporary lodgings. I looked for the effect of the crash which had disturbed me, but the pill-box had so many chunks knocked off it that I was unable to determine where the shell had struck. I met a transport driver and begged a match.

"Jerry's played hell all night, ain't he, mate," said the driver.

"He damn well has," I replied.

"Any shelling by the dump?" he asked.

"Can't say," I answered. "Haven't been near since last night." The dump was near the end of the communication trench and was a notoriously dangerous spot.

"Suppose I shall find out pretty soon." He started his engine and went down the road at a brisk speed.

I walked quietly in the homeward direction. Everything seemed so peaceful. Not a shell or a gun could be heard. The warm sunshine made me feel glad that I was alive. If only the war would end. How often that wish had entered my mind. But there was no hope. The end seemed as far away as when I had first enlisted. It could go on for years. There was no valid reason why it should not. Months of concentrated effort only yielded two or three miles of new ground at the most. How long then would it be before the enemy was pushed back into his own territory?—and even then they could fight indefinitely, just like France was fighting now. I could find no sign of the cloud with the silver lining which everyone was singing. I might possibly be trudging in and out of the trenches when in the normal run of things I should be viewing the prospect of becoming a grandfather. The only qualification was to bear a charmed life in the meantime.

This particular road had been constructed after the recent advance and was almost wholly comprised of tree trunks laid side by side. I came across some of the results of the previous night's strafe, a smashed limber strewn over a considerable area, and mules lying dead. Here and there a great gap in the tree trunks where a direct hit had been registered. A little farther along I found the bodies of two men drawn to the side of the road, with a ground-sheet covering their faces. I drew the ground-sheet aside, and disclosed the features of two signallers attached to "D" company, whom I knew very well indeed. Their bodies were bloody, but their faces calm and composed in death. The sight of these dead friends lying stiff and silent aroused within me the usual feeling of the tragedy of war and the utter uselessness of it all.

I could picture those gunners of the German battery not so very far away. Perhaps just at this moment they would be peacefully sleeping, or maybe writing to their loved ones after their night's work of firing so many shells on a certain target, blissfully unconscious of what they had done, happy because they were enjoying a few hours' rest; and here was the target and the result of their handiwork. Two mutilated corpses that once were men.

Reverently I covered their faces and went my way.

CHAPTER XIX

AN OUTPOST

THE battalion had moved from the old front line, and I found them in huts on the far slope of Kemmel Hill. Rumours of a move to the country near St. Omer were very prevalent, and everyone seemed happy and relieved. Then the weather changed, and it rained so incessantly that the intended journey was temporarily postponed.

This filled us with misgivings, which were realized after the rain had persisted for three days, for we were instructed to parade in fighting order, and after being equipped with rations and gumboots, we were again bound for the trenches. Directly we reached the extreme point of the new roads we began to flounder in a morass of mud and water, varying in depth from two or three inches to as many feet, and progress was both difficult and painful. On the first night and the day following, we occupied the support line. It was not the same trench as previously, being much more to the right and nearer Vierstraate. There were posts in front, and I was detailed to relieve one of the Lewis gun positions. Shorty was obliged to remain with the company, although I believe that he would gladly have accompanied us.

AN OUTPOST

A local advance had quite recently been made and the posts were pushed out some hundreds of yards in front of the main line. To reach them, we ploughed through mud and barbed wire and every conceivable obstacle, and the firing of machine-guns kept us in a constant state of anxiety. There were several positions to relieve and quite a number of us followed the guide in single file, stopping for a while as each post was relieved. Eventually we came to the position that I was to occupy. It was a shallow piece of trench about two yards long and two feet wide, and four of us had to get into it. But before we could do that the party to be relieved had to get out. They were stuck in the mud and only by pulling hard could we release them.

"Christ help yer, chum, it's the wust night I've ever had," whispered one of the men.

Once in the trench we became in a similar plight. The mud was deep and binding, and we could barely move. The more we struggled the tighter we stuck, and we were entirely out of action so far as being able to defend ourselves. The gun was quite all right, but it was impossible to use it. We had not a single bomb between us and we were over a quarter of a mile from the front line, with the possibility of an attack being launched. We were of less use to the British cause than a man driving a tramload of munition workers. Thirty yards away was a German machine-gun which swept the top of the trench so frequently that we were forced to keep our heads below the parapet.

At first we tried the expedient of scooping up handfuls of mud and slinging it to the rear, but water was trickling in from somewhere and making more mud, and we soon gave up the task and settled down in a stooping position with our arms wedged tightly into the sides of the trench. From this position I kept slipping into the mud and struggling out again, and my arms wore channels in the earth so that every minute the difficulty of keeping off the muddy bottom became greater. Day came and we still crouched there, unable to stand upright because of the shallowness of the hole. Sometimes I dozed and awoke to find I was sitting and sinking in the mud, and it would require the helpful grip of another to enable me to regain my former position. We talked and groused and tried to be cheerful, but there was little humour to be found in squatting there. Fortunately we were not subjected to enemy shell-fire. We were too close to his own posts for that to be attempted, but our batteries were firing short pretty frequently and they gave us many shocks which had been intended for the German garrison.

The contour of the ground was such that without moving we could see the bits of trenches to the left of the post, and we saw that the men stationed in those holes were having an anxious time with our own guns. From one place several men were seen to crawl away and occupy a shell-hole some yards to the rear, and we watched with bated breath while they safely negotiated the short distance under the very noses of the enemy. That day was the slowest I have ever experienced. We amused ourselves by guessing the time. At ten o'clock one man thought it was about two. At twelve another guessed five o'clock. At half-past one I thought the watch must have lost a couple of hours through the damp.

We ate our food, but it was unpalatable, being impregnated with mud, and we had nothing whereby we could boil water for tea. Grateful we were that the post was to be of only twenty-four hours' duration, and we lived in hope that nothing untoward would occur when night came on. Our hopes were soon dispelled, for even as dusk was approaching a fierce drumfire commenced on the extreme left of our vision and high in the air floated a single red light. It was the German appeal for retaliation.

The cannonade which followed must have been the cause of a British distress rocket being fired, and more guns took up the challenge, and more enemy red lights appeared, gradually spreading along the front, ever nearer our position, where we waited and watched with dry lips and nerves strained to breaking-point. At length the dreaded light flared up immediately in front and then to the right, and presently we could hear the avalanche of shells pouring over our heads to burst well to the rear. Soon more British distress signals were being fired on either side. They were gorgeous fireworks, being showers of coloured lights, and were impossible to mistake.

We feared for the barrage which must follow, for our faith in the batteries had been sadly undermined by the shortness of their range earlier in the day; but our fears were groundless. The guns joined in the mêlée, and, not only was a perfect range maintained, but they provided such a solid curtain of fire that we experienced a most comforting feeling of safety and immunity from attack. The machine-gun in front was silenced and we were able to watch unmolested the devastating effect of the barrage. The lighter calibre guns were trained on the ground some fifty yards ahead, the heavies were pouring their quota on the rear trenches and the roads of communication, and in the gathering gloom we could just distinguish the shapes of several pill-boxes which were being subjected to a terrific bombardment by guns of at least 9.2 calibre. A couple of hours went by and the shelling had wellnigh ceased. The German machine-gunner signalized that he was alive by firing a long burst. Then the relief came. We were pulled out of the hole in the manner of our predecessors, and I stood on the top numbed and aching, but not for long. That machine-gun was likely to get going again. In a few minutes we had put a comfortable distance between us and the wretched post. Back in the supports I discovered that the company had been relieved and had gone, and I was not sorry, for it meant greater freedom of movement. As a natural sequence to the severe gunfire, the roads were being shelled at various points, and having learned a great deal on the last journey out I suggested passing the night in a pill-box. This was heartily approved, and after finding one to suit our convenience we settled down for the night.

. . . . . .

The division was being relieved by the Australians, and near our camp at Dranoutre an Anzac battalion was clearing up preparatory to marching to the trenches. Shorty and I walked over and made the acquaintance of some of these splendid fellows. We talked with them about the part of the front which they were taking over and, as is usual with infantry regiments, they wanted to know how the shelling was, and what state the trenches were in, and the location of posts, etc.

So much has been written about the glorious Anzacs that I was not a little surprised to find their demeanour quite akin to ours. They did not like holding trenches, they detested shelling, and they abhorred "going over the top". They were fed-up with France, they had experienced enough of war to last them, and they wanted peace and the country down under. All the rubbish that was written of super-men who liked fighting and bayonet charges and bombing stunts boiled down to the one common matter-of-fact statement that the plain ordinary man of whatever nationality, or origin, detested the very name of war. Only a lunatic could find solace in the doctrine of blood and more blood.

Collectively, an army consists of a number of units under one control, with but one aim—victory at any cost. Individually, it consists of plain John Smith, or Herr Schmidt, with brains that think, with bodies that can feel pain, with but one life which they wish to live to its fullest extent. The plain official statement that the Blankshires or the Bavarians have captured Hill 20, means that many hundreds of men possessing aims and ambitions other than war, fearing death and mangled limbs, have faced bayonets and shell-fire, and although suffering agonies of mind have obeyed the call of discipline. I have talked with German prisoners, with French soldiers, with Colonials, and last but not least, Scottish, Irish, and Welsh, and never did I find a man who liked the atmosphere of war. The healthy life of soldiering might suit many, but in the hearts of those who must suffer most, war is hell. How then can we reconcile this state of mind with the simple truth that war, like the poor, will always be with us? It is not that we do not know any different. It is not that the masses are uneducated and cannot think for themselves. The masses provide nine-tenths of an army at war, and suffer nine-tenths of the blood sacrifice. This being so, the common peoples of the world should have nine-tenths of the say as to whether they shall endure it any longer. Unfortunately the masses have too often allowed their patriotism to be imposed on, and by their apathy have become the willing slaves of the war lord .

CHAPTER XX

RESTING

For several weeks the Worcesters had been living in various villages many miles behind the line, and a stay of a fortnight's duration was made in the pleasant hamlet of Nielles Les Blequin. We enjoyed a good time, and although there were many parades and much tackle-cleaning to do, we could soldier with an easier mind than was possible in the trenches.

Work usually ended about half-past three and after tea the usual trek began into the centre of the village, where the playing of the drum and fife and bugle bands was the chief attraction. It became quite an imposing affair, and the inhabitants were never tired of watching the khaki-clad musicians as they paraded the square.

"D" Company was billeted in the inevitable barn, and Shorty and I found refuge in a loft which was reached by climbing a decrepit stepladder with several rungs missing. It was easy enough to negotiate when wearing just ordinary walking-out dress, but when clad in full marching order, as we often were, it would have tested the agility of a monkey. Once inside, however, the loft was commodious and comfortable, and its chief importance to this narrative is that it witnessed the entry of Tanky into the gun-team.

A new order had come into force to the effect that a Lewis gun-team must have an N.C.O. as section leader. This was communicated to me with the suggestion that I should overcome the difficulty by taking a stripe, and as I had no desire to do so, Tanky, who was a lance-jack, was sent to make up the deficiency, and henceforth I must serve as a number one under him.

Tanky was a Black Country man and proud of it. He was short, and possessed a rotundity which no amount of marching could reduce. His face was podgy, his eyes full of merriment, and his good temper invulnerable. Tanky liked many things, but his stomach for preference. His rations were supplemented with innumerable parcels from home, and they contained anything from pork pie to whisky. Tanky's better half in the far-away Black Country knew her man, and with that proverbial Black Country faith in the stomach, meant getting "summut" down him. Tanky was a distinct acquisition to the gun-team. His dry humour and happy disposition was like a tonic, and we rapidly absorbed him into the inner recesses of our confidences.

One of the many diversions which occurred during our period of rest was when arrangements were made to take the battalion in motor-lorries to Boulogne, some forty miles distant. Whether the idea was to give us a day's outing, or whether it was considered we could do with a thorough scouring with sea water, I cannot say, but we welcomed the trip with open arms. We were due to meet the lorries at a point about four miles from where we were staying, and clad in walking-out dress, and carrying ground-sheets, we set out gaily on this unexpected adventure. Arrived at the starting point, it was decided that we might need our water-bottles, and so we were marched the four miles to billets and back to the lorries again. This was an unhappy augury and was the cause of much swearing, for we were already dog-tired and the day was well advanced. Some of the men wanted to forgo the pleasure, but it was not one of those kind of trips where you could change your mind at the last moment, and I rather think that if it had been decided that we must fetch the remainder of our kit in instalments we should still have been compelled to go.

Apparently everything was now satisfactory, for we were allowed to climb into the lorries, and the excursion began. Such a little matter as a twelve miles' enforced march was not wont to disturb the tranquillity of a whole battalion, and for three solid hours we rode through village after village cheering like brakeloads of children on a Sunday School outing.

To those who had expected a joyful afternoon in a big French seaport came a blow, big and sure. With extra strong field-glasses we might have seen the colour of the brick buildings that showed faintly in the distance. But humans are ever ungrateful.

Here we were by the side of the sea, with a portion of the beach reserved for our exclusive use, splashing about to our heart's content, and men were grousing because military police kept guard on either side. They wanted to roam to their heart's content. Maybe they would have liked to imagine just for a few hours that the war was over, and that they were again at Blackpool, or Weston, or Brighton, or wherever they used to spend their summer vacations; but those military police. Even a battalion naked to a man, with nothing but tattoo marks to awaken suspicions of militarism, could not look on them and pretend there was not a war on.

Notwithstanding these incidents with which we could not see eye to eye, we enjoyed ourselves thoroughly, and after a few hours of inhaling the ozone, and vainly trying to obtain a glimpse of those white cliffs which are for ever England, we re-entered the lorries and sang away the forty miles to billets.

Soon after this interlude we were given another ride in motor-lorries; a rather long ride which finally landed us within measurable distance of the line. It was on the outskirts of Meteren, and Meteren was a place beloved by troops because of its capacity for supplying the needs of the moment. Here "D" Company was quartered in sheds attached to an estaminet. The proprietor also owned hop-fields and a farm. It was hop-picking time when we arrived, and men strolling through the hop-fields noticed that the owner had a pleasant habit of visiting his workers with great jugs of beer. "D" Company started hop-picking after parades. Butter churning was another pastime for anyone who was hard-up and possessed a thirst, but it was a monotonous task, and after the first hour of swinging the flat tub which served the purpose, and after sundry peeps inside to see how much butter had formed and finding only a few yellow floating spots, the amateur churner usually remembered he had his buttons to clean. The non-appearance of the farmer with the jug often assisted in a speedy arrival at this decision. At night-time, much of the company paraded inside the estaminet and drank pints of beer until eight o'clock, which was turning out time, and then they adjourned to the estaminet keeper's kitchen, and with due caution drank more pints until ten o'clock, which was turning out time again.

A very great source of annoyance to us was the difficulty of obtaining French bread. At one time, if the day's issue was meagre, it was easily and cheaply supplemented by purchasing a quantity from the villagers, but the authorities had put a stop to this, and now it was an offence to sell bread to British troops. It became necessary to make arrangements with some willing housewife to reserve a certain amount, and then when it was dark a secret visit would be made and the bread surreptitiously removed. Ofttimes a man could be seen returning innocently to billets with his chest bulging in two or three places, and happy were they who could boast a regular source of supply. I once walked five miles to a village where we had stayed some months before, and I called at a place which had billeted some of "D" Company.

I led off with the usual formula:

"Any du pan, Madame?"

She eyed me suspiciously.

"No du pan, compree perlice, no bon."

I thought then that I might do better if I claimed previous acquaintance.

"Ah, Madame, compree Worcesters, billet here, cushy, bon time." I exhausted all my scanty stock of French and was just beginning to think I had made an impression when the good lady recalled a detail of our former visit.

"Me compree Worcesters. No pay, no bon."

It had so happened that during our sojourn there we had not been paid, but I got some bread nevertheless.

Most of the inhabitants of Meteren spoke fairly good English, for they had seen much of our troops. The British had swept the Germans out of Meteren in 1914, and the villagers had not forgotten. Graves were scattered about in the most unexpected places: one was in a garden, another in the centre of a field of wheat, but wherever they lay they were kept supplied with fresh flowers by the people who lived near.

Never did we imagine that the Germans would again overrun that pleasant countryside, but in 1918 Meteren once more came under the heel of the despoiler.

This comfortable spell out of the line was rapidly drawing to a close, and one day we moved into a camp which was to be the reserve quarters for the sector facing Klein Zillebeke, and quite near to Hill 60. The latter place was now some considerable distance within the British lines, and motor-lorries could convey troops right up to the famous hill without coming under the observation of the enemy. A huge crater caused by the mine explosion had been converted into billets, capable of housing a company, and Lewis gun sections were kept employed on the crest for anti-aircraft work. Our gun-team was so employed on several occasions, but we never had the satisfaction of bringing one down, and it is an infinitely harder task than most people imagine.

Once, in supports, a suspicious-looking craft was observed flying overhead. It was rather misty and

Shorty pushed the gun through an iron loop which was attached to a post for that purpose.

"It's a Jerry, all right," said Shorty.

"I think it belongs to we," Tanky replied.

They argued for a time and the plane came lower and lower, but still we could not distinguish the markings. Suddenly Shorty fired a burst shouting that he knew it was a Jerry, and immediately other machine-guns in the vicinity which had been similarly perplexed opened on the plane and the pilot, thoroughly alarmed, dropped a couple of lights and sped quickly away. A couple of hours later we were being questioned as to who had been firing on a Belgian aeroplane.

Preparations were being made for an attack on a fairly wide front, and our division was to form the right flank of the advance. This involved peculiar difficulties, for the flank is invariably exposed to enfilade fire. Our task would be a moderate one, according to the details which we were given. We were to push forward for a distance of one thousand yards and we were in the scheme only to divert the attention of the enemy from the more serious operations to be carried out on our left. It was to be purely a game of bluff. No serious obstacles were expected, and it was anticipated that we should be safely settled in the new line soon after dawn.

Some of us had problems apart from the ordinary business of attack.

The company officer had sent for me and had expounded a rather startling proposition. It was to the effect that would I care to volunteer for a battle patrol, and while I was pondering this weighty subject, he followed it up with the remark: "Well, it is hardly a matter of volunteering, you have been selected." So that was that. The job was simplicity itself. All that the selected gunners were required to do was to wait until the advancing line had reached its objective, and then to march up and down the new "No Man's Land" sweeping up sundry snipers and bombers who by some mischance had been left behind. That the said snipers and bombers might have a serious objection to being swept up by half a Lewis gun-team was another matter and had not been included in the programme.

Before this attack was made we were to be treated to a spell in the trenches for a preliminary look round. Accordingly, we left the lorries at Hill 60 and found much evidence of what was to be expected in the course of a few days. As at Messines, so here, were guns in countless numbers, with their ugly noses pointing in the direction of Klein Zillebeke, while stacks of shells were encountered everywhere we walked. The gun-team made itself comfortable in a pill-box in the supports. A certain amount of hostile shelling was taking place, and Tanky commented on the number of "duds" which were being fired. Unfortunately the "duds" proved to be mustard gas, and this we realized when we were in such a condition of sneezing and coughing that it became a matter of extreme difficulty to keep the gas-masks in position Gas has a nasty habit of clinging to low-lying areas and the inside of buildings, and we were forced to evacuate the pill-box and brave the elements in the trench outside. During the next morning a wonderful discovery was made. Turnips were growing in profusion around the trenches. How they came there was no concern of ours. They were turnips and that was sufficient. Shorty, who was an authority on matters horticultural, pronounced them good and fit for human consumption, and the top was knocked off a petrol tin and a great boiling of turnips placed therein. The result was so satisfying that it was decided to improve on the brew. Pork-and-beans, bully, biscuits, and meat were all tipped into the petrol tin and we achieved a meal which, if it was not exactly like mother used to make, was probably as good as she could have made given similar ingredients and circumstances.

The front line, which was on the crest of a ridge, gave a splendid view of the immediate country in the possession of the enemy. With the naked eye several churches could be seen quite distinctly and far-distant chimney-stacks were smoking furiously. I looked many times through field-glasses at apparently sleepy villages a few miles away, but never did I see the slightest sign of life, only the smoking stacks and the flashing of guns.

The effect of our own gun-fire was remarkable. Roads and strategic points were being systematically shelled, and although only a minor bombardment was in progress, the country was literally plastered with shell-bursts. I wondered what would be the effect when from those odd nooks and corners the concealed guns joined in the attack.

Little of note occurred during the preliminary look-round, and after three days we came back to the reserve camp to prepare for the greater trial which was now so near.

CHAPTER XXI

THE MENIN ROAD BATTLE

It was the night before we moved to the trenches for the "push", and the divisional band had arrived to entertain the troops. The sergeant-majors and sergeants were possessed of a barrel of beer, and they formed a boisterous party in a corner of the camp. I strolled away from the tents for I felt moody and wished to be alone.

The band was playing "When you come to the end of a perfect day", and the tune seemed peculiarly affecting. I felt strangely apprehensive and not a little home-sick. For a full year I had been escaping death by inches and I wondered how long it could last. I wanted to shake the hands of those I loved. How good it would have seemed if someone from the home-land could have passed by then. No matter if he had been a one-time enemy, I could have fallen on him and embraced him.

I tried to concentrate my thoughts on the distant future when war should be no more and the accursed trenches were only a memory, but I could see no future. I could not look beyond the next two days. My life, and the lives of thousands of other men, were but the playthings of the moment. In a couple of days, perhaps less, the acres of Klein Zillebeke would be stained with the blood of those who were now listening to the music of a popular melody. In forty-eight hours their fresh young bodies would have started to rot. It was no idle premonition, no exaggerated view of what might be. It was a stark raving fact that twenty per cent of the men were not expected to be living in two days from now, and even though thirty, forty, or even fifty per cent of the combatants are left lying stiff and motionless, the war lords, with eyes uplifted, can recant the words of the old poem: "But 'twas a glorious victory."

For a long time I mused thus. The band had completed their programme and had played "The King". The raucous laughter of the sergeants came echoing across the ground. The bugles rang out the weird notes of the "Last Post". It was time to return.

Spoilbank was on the side of the canal that runs near Ypres. It had been excavated and converted into a wonderful series of subterranean tunnels which provided a safe reserve for thousands of troops. It was honeycombed with passages which contained wire beds, and a central roadway which led from end to end afforded room for the rapid transit of whole battalions. The canal was but a canal in name. Most of its water had long since drained away and the locks were broken with much shelling. Running parallel with the side of the embankment was a trench-board track, elevated a foot or more above the ground. The track was a target for German gunners, who pounded it often and with many direct hits. It was constantly being renewed, and smashed, and again renewed.

Certain engineers had lived for months in Spoilbank, and to follow their advice was to follow the road to safety. Their advice was: "Keep inside, but if you have to go out, run," and many a man could be seen doing a quarter of a mile in record time across that dreaded stadium.

This, then, was the place which the battalion came to on the afternoon of the 19th of September. The interior was crowded to its uttermost capacity, for several units were waiting, ready to march to the assembly trenches for the attack on the morrow.

Tanky and I sat in the corner of a passage jammed with humanity. Shorty was with us and was rather jubilant because we were not in the first wave.

"Being the reserve company will be the cushiest thing we've had," he said. "The others will get it hot because the ground's so open, and it's a pound to a penny that the machine-guns will be going hell for leather."

"How about our job, you don't call that cushy, do you?" I said.

"I'd forgotten that," replied Shorty. "Of course, you're on the battle patrol. Nasty job, and I shouldn't advise you to take any risks. Mopping up shell-holes is no mug's game, I'll warrant."

"It's cushy enough for we," said Tanky, who had not been detailed for the patrol; "that's unless one of the other companies get smashed, and then we're in it up to the neck."

"What do you reckon to be doing in this picture?" I asked of Shorty.

"Nothing, old man," he replied.

"What are you carrying?"

"Nothing bar my kit."

"Lucky devil," I said, thinking of the gun and ammunition which we had to struggle with to the trenches.

"It's like this, you chaps," said Shorty. "I've taken that darned gun over till I'm sick of the sight of it, and it's about time I carried something a bit more congenial. I'll tell you what I'll do. Give me your ration bag and I'll get that up there for you."

"Good old Shorty," said I, for the bag of rations had been something of a problem. They had only just been received and it was proposed to divide them early in the morning.

"I suppose we can trust him with the grub, can't we?" said Tanky, with a chuckle.

"We can till he gets hungry, but that won't happen till we've got the bag back," I replied.

We continued chatting in this manner until the order was given to prepare to move; then picking up our gear, we somewhat reluctantly left the pleasant shelter of the dugouts. Coming directly from the well-lit passages, the darkness outside was impenetrable. It was raining heavily and some confusion occurred when we pushed our way out and found the side of the embankment crowded with men awaiting orders.

"Lead on," cried many voices, for they knew full well the reputation of the canal side. We began to move slowly along the duckboards The flashing of many guns from across the canal was blinding, and walking a track which was narrow and could not be seen was like walking a tight-rope. On either side was mud, and at every few yards a halt became necessary while some unfortunate was dragged gasping and cursing on to the track again.

The duckboards ran in a snake-like fashion and it became an utter impossibility to keep from stepping in the wrong direction. After I had fallen two or three times, I tried walking through the mud, but it was deep and binding and I was in danger of becoming exhausted, so that I was glad to climb back on to the track and take my chance with the others. The roar of a shell passed over our heads, and the explosion not very far away increased the agony which we were enduring. Foot by foot we crept along and at last reached a point known as Oaf trench, and here the going became easier. Soon after midnight we reached the assembly trenches. It was deemed advisable to get away from the actual trench, and we lay in shell-holes among the tree stumps of a battered wood. The next few hours were hideous and nerve-wracking, for we were subjected to the fire of heavy guns which threatened at times to make our position untenable. Great pieces of shrapnel, capable of slicing a man in halves, hurtled over us, and whiz-bangs scattered the earth in all directions. Almost before we expected it the barrage had opened, and for some moments the hell that was let loose caused my nerves to go to pieces, but this was a common feeling with troops awaiting the moment of attack, and was but a temporary condition.

The commencement of the barrage was the signal for "D" Company to follow up the attacking waves, and we made for the trench which led to the front line. The German counter-barrage crashed on this trench, and was so effective that there were many casualties almost immediately. I was following the tail end of another platoon, and just as they disappeared round a bend in the trench there came a fearful explosion. I paused for a few seconds and then carried on. Where the shell had burst resembled a human slaughter-house. Several men were lying dead, their bodies mangled as though they had been savaged by some prehistoric beast. One fellow stood against the side of the trench. Half of his face was gone and the inside of the other cheek plainly visible. I knew him well and he tried to smile, but I was too shocked to speak or smile in return. Another man was gazing with horror at a bleeding forearm from which the hand was missing. I hurried on to a point where trenches ran both left and right, and I was uncertain which to take. A very tall man, his face deathly pale, his hands gripping a great red patch on his chest, staggered to the entrance of the right-hand trench and gradually slipped to the ground, blocking the path. He had come from the left trench, so I judged that to be the one we should take, and, followed immediately by the two who were taking part in the battle patrol, we dashed through an inferno of bursting shells and flying debris. On the ground at the back of the trench lay the bodies of men of the Machine-Gun Corps who had been killed while assisting the barrage. One particular gun and team reminded me of the grim tableau of a waxwork show. The passage was becoming more difficult. Trench-boards and corrugated iron sheets were being blown into the air. In places it was blocked by mounds of earth and piles of burst sandbags, and to make matters worse we had not met a live person to give us the right direction.

We decided to return, and once again ran the gauntlet of that fearful barrage, escaping death I know not how. We reached the cross-roads and found a barricade of dead and dying which completely blocked the right-hand trench. I could imagine what had happened. The wounded, pouring back from the advancing waves, had found the tall pale-faced man lying in their path, and those that were able stepped over him; but there must have come men who were too badly wounded and exhausted to negotiate the obstacle, and they had simply piled themselves one above the other in a last desperate struggle to reach safety. Stretcher-bearers were trying to disentangle one particular man who seemed more alive than the others, but their task was a big and trying one, for every movement brought forth a chorus of pitiful groans from the ghastly heap.

An officer, white and agitated, appeared above the trench and, seeing us, cried: "For God's sake hurry, you will be wanted soon."

I pushed the gun over and climbed out, and thirty yards beyond we had passed through the barrage. I glanced behind and saw the shells tearing the trench to pieces, and I thought of that rampart of dead and dying and those patient stretcher-bearers.

We found some of "D" Company sheltering in a concreted gun-pit, over which was an arch like a small railway tunnel. A man, disembowelled, was dying in agony, and helplessly we watched his struggles until a last convulsive shudder told us that his suffering had ended.

The succession of horrors was confusing my mind. I was cool, yet had a strange idea that the end was near. The roar of the batteries was unceasing and a stream of enemy shells were passing over us to burst on the fateful trench we had just left.

Several hundreds of yards away the barrage was creeping steadily and remorselessly over the enemy lines, and the first two companies of the battalion could be seen following in its wake. Columns of earth were rising behind them, for the Germans were concentrating on preventing the arrival of reinforcements. The scene was impressive. That men can advance through such a hell when their very instincts must be shrieking out for safety! But there is no turning back. Discipline will ever conquer fear.

Even as we were watching the progress of the battle a huge shell burst near the entrance of the gun-pit, and when the smoke had cleared and I had recovered my wits, I found that my two patrol partners were lying dead. This occurrence filled the remainder with panic and we dashed from the gun-pit and sought shelter in holes and bits of trenches. I was relieved to find Tanky sitting in a corner smoking a "Woodbine".

"Where yer bin?" he asked quietly.

I told him the situation as regards the patrol.

"Can't do anything till they send a runner," he replied. "They'll soon send when they want yer."

That, of course, was the original order. We were to wait until instructions reached us.

"Seen anything of Shorty?" Tanky asked.

That reminded me. I had not seen him since the

previous night. I wondered if he was still alive, and where.

"He's got our rations," continued Tanky.

"It will be a case if he don't turn up. No grub till to-morrow," I answered.

In this small piece of trench were three gunners, several company men, and an officer who had only lately joined the battalion after seeing service in the East. The officer confessed that he had lost his batman, who was carrying his rations, so I opened my emergency tin of bully and shared it. This warmed up his confidence.

"Should you call this affair hot, or merely ordinary?" he asked.

"Red hot," I replied. "If it gets any hotter we're done."

"I'm glad to hear that, for a repetition of this every day would be a little too much," he answered.

The opened tin of bully had sharpened the appetite of one of the riflemen and he decided to go and inquire where his rations had gone; and a few hours later he was being passed through a Casualty Clearing Station on his way to England. We knew that shrapnel must have burst pretty close to him, for it had dropped well in the direction he had taken.

After a certain time had elapsed another man evinced a desire to follow him, and once he had passed the range of our vision we saw him no more until a day in the distant future, when he rejoined us the proud possessor of a gold stripe.

Naturally, these happenings were unknown to us at the time, or otherwise they would have proved a deterrent. Within the next few minutes the officer had left us, and we knew not the reason of his absence until his name was officially included in the list of dead.

We were lying in a dreary position. The attack was finished, but the attackers could no longer be seen owing to the contour of the ground. Nearby was a stagnant pool containing a dead German, and the murky water was stained a crimson hue. I kept looking at him and wondered how long he had been there and if he was married, and whether he had been thrown in, or had crawled there to die alone. Twenty yards away lay a man with both legs torn off below the knees. He was an officer's servant, a quiet, inoffensive sort of chap, well liked by everyone, and perhaps a little above the average type of infantryman. I had passed him coming to the trench and he had asked after the stretcher-bearers, but I had not the heart to tell him that they were overwhelmed with cases, and that he had little hope of being carried away for many hours.

Perhaps it would be proper to explain that the stretcher-bearers, of which so much is mentioned, were ordinary privates trained in first-aid methods, and were unconnected with the Royal Army Medical Corps. The stretcher-bearers of that unit did not often come into the front trenches, at least so far as my battalion was concerned. The wounded, as a general rule, were conveyed to a point some distance behind the fighting line and there handed over to the care of the R.A.M.C. Stretcher-bearing was a task which demanded both strength and courage, and volunteers were distinctly lacking.

Just before midday the long-expected runner came

from the advanced line and inquired for the battle patrol. The patrol had been washed out, he said, because the front was badly enfiladed. We were, however, to take the place of a gun-team which had been wiped out. Thereupon Tanky commandeered a couple of riflemen to bring up the team to a respectable strength, and we followed the runner to the new line.

I was amazed to see that no attempt was being made to keep under cover. Men were walking about the top as though they were miles behind the lines. A considerable number of holes had been dug haphazard, but there was no communication between any two of them. The locality was not that of the "preliminary look-round". A thousand yards away was a ridge which limited the vision, and I presumed that for the present the Germans must have retired well beyond the ridge, otherwise we should have been heavily fired upon. A few pill-boxes were scattered about in front and the land seemed marshy midway to the ridge. On the left were the dwarfed stumps of a once not inconsiderable wood, and beyond that the country opened out to permit of a wide field of fire.

Things went along pretty smoothly for an hour or so, and then came the roar of a salvo of shells which sent us scuttling into the holes. Later in the afternoon we could see enemy troops as they passed by a gap on the ridge, and orders were given to fire as they exposed themselves. They were evidently massing at various points prior to counter-attacking.

Just before dusk, with very little artillery preparation, the Germans commenced an assault. It was ill-advised, for they had much open ground to cover, and even as they debouched from the left portion of the ridge, machine-gun and rifle fire swept the slope which they must traverse, and the barrage which followed speedily convinced them that the attempt was hopeless. They retired quickly, leaving behind a considerable number of casualties.

I had fired two magazines when a great piece of shrapnel struck the gun, completely disabling it. It was beyond immediate repair and Tanky decided to fetch another. He went back to where we had left the remnants of the company and for a couple of hours I wondered if he had been hit. The shelling was becoming heavy and it was essential for every man to keep well down; but in the midst of the strafe came Tanky, hot and excited. He had borrowed another gun from somewhere. I tried it and found it defective, but with partially stripping the gun we discovered a minor error which was speedily corrected.

A fairly quiet night ensued, and in the early morning the mail and rations arrived. It was remarkable how letters and parcels followed us to the most inaccessible places; but, of course, where men are sent, food must follow, and the post generally came with it.

I received from home the local newspaper, and opening it, found underlined, in a column devoted to those local men who had made the great sacrifice, the name of a friend who had met his death somewhere near Ypres. It was strangely incongruous that I should have my attention drawn to it just at a time when I was not at all sure but that my own name would, in the course of a week, be included in that selfsame column. Colour was lent to this by the crashing of a British protective barrage which signalized dawn by peppering the ground in front of the German lines.

For twenty-four hours we had existed on nothing but our emergency rations, and it was with very great satisfaction we noted that to-day's issue was abnormally large. This was rather puzzling at first until we remembered that the company had suffered many casualties. How many we did not know, but judging by the amount of food sent to us there must have been very few other mouths to feed.

The hole which Tanky and I occupied was too small to accommodate more than two and allow for freedom of movement, so the remainder had settled in a piece of trench that ran at rightangles to ours. About six feet of earth separated the two holes, and communication was kept up by shouting across. Early in the afternoon a German aeroplane, flying very low, appeared over our position. He was obviously observing the formation of the new line. From some distance away an officer cried out to us to open fire, and somewhat reluctantly I disposed of a magazine, but apparently without effect, for after circling the immediate front, he made a detour to his own lines.

Some hours later the enemy artillery became active and a whizbang battery commenced, directing the fire of one of its guns unpleasantly near our little trench. At first we did not take a great deal of notice, but it gradually dawned on us that the shots were being observed and that we were the target.

Every two or three minutes we could distinguish the report of the gun, followed immediately by a crash in our vicinity. One burst near enough to smother us with stones and earth, and it began to cause serious anxiety.

"This is through firing the perishin' gun," shouted a voice from the other trench. "I'm getting out."

I looked over and saw one of the gunners scramble out and make for a shell-hole. A few minutes later we heard him shout, and saw him crawling to the rear with one leg badly injured.

"Bang" went the gun and "crash" came the shell, with horrible regularity, sometimes quite close, sometimes a little further away, and we knew we were faced with death unless the infernal thing should stop.

We piled the rations about us to ward off pieces of shrapnel which flew into the trench, and our conversation developed into a strange assortment of positive and negative phrases.

"D'ye think he'll get us, Tanky?"

"No. I think we're safe enough, do you?"

"He will if he keeps on."

Then another shell would burst, and Tanky would say: "Don't seem to have much of a chance, do we?"

"Oh, I don't know He isn't obliged to hit us," I would reply.

Tanky had a tin of Maconochie over his heart and bully-beef and jam alongside, while I balanced half a loaf where I guessed my lungs were. It was ridiculous but might reduce an otherwise mortal wound to a superficial one.

"I've been in some perishin' 'oles, but this is a licker," said Tanky. "Can't we get out?"

"We're holding the line," I answered.

"Got to wait for the packet, I suppose."

"Can't go without showing blood, that's very evident."

He lapsed into quietness.

"What are you doing, Tanky?" I asked.

"Only praying, mate. Don't seem much else left; do you?"

"Do what?"

"Pray."

"I've been praying ever since that gun opened," I replied.

"Perhaps he's praying to hit us."

"Good Lord, Tanky, what a thing to say."

And still the gun fired and the shells burst near, while we crouched, and hoped and prayed that it would cease, and then came the moment which we knew was inevitable. We heard the report of the gun and instinctively cowered lower. There was a blinding explosion and a moment later we were half-buried by a part of the trench. I was semi-stunned, but struggled to free myself.

"Tanky, all right?" I spluttered.

"God's strewth! I thought I was a gonner," said Tanky. "Them chaps have got it, though."

The shell had struck the piece of ground which divided us and had burst forward. I bent over and saw a headless body.

A wild piercing scream came from the trench.

"Come on," said Tanky, "let's get across."

We crawled over the gap made by the shell.

One man lay at the bottom of the trench with eyes wide open and a terrible hole in his throat. Another was at the far end screaming and moaning alternately.

Leaning against the trench was the man from Walsall, dazed but otherwise uninjured.

"Look! Look!" he said, pointing at the decapitated gunner.

"Never mind him, now. What's the matter with that chap?" asked Tanky.

We knew the wounded man as George. One of his eyes was bleeding profusely.

"Where's your dressing, George?" I asked.

"Leave my leg alone," he screamed.

"It's broke," said Tanky. "See how it's doubled up."

"Take me away," cried George, piteously.

"We can't yet," Tanky answered. "We'll be getting the stretcher-bearers here just now. Hi, over there, pass the word for stretcher-bearers."

With some difficulty I tied the bandage over his eye. He was groaning horribly, but neither of us knew what to do with a broken limb.

It suddenly occurred to me that the whizbang gun had ceased firing.

"I knew they meant getting us," said Tanky, when I mentioned it.

"Stretcher-bearers coming in a few minutes," yelled a voice from across the ground.

It was getting dusk and the general shelling rapidly increased to such violence that we were forced to crawl back to the gun in case of emergency. We found it choked with earth and we partly stripped it and cleaned the bolt and other vital working parts, but even then it would not fire a round.

"Damn fine thing if he comes over," said Tanky.

Darkness came, and with the subsidence of the shelling the stretcher-bearers got George away.

The best news we received was that we were being relieved, and this presented us with a further problem, for the gun, spare parts, and a dozen magazines had to be carried away.

I found an officer and explained the position, and he suggested that we should take out as much as possible and leave the remainder.

"Get the dead men's identity discs," he concluded.

We were able to procure the one disc, but the extent of the injuries of the second man made it impossible.

An hour later the relief battalion came in and, leaving our dead in their ready-made graves, we hastened back to the original line.

Once out of the danger zone I felt wonderfully cheerful. The joy of having passed safely through such a crisis was intoxicating, but back at the camp I suffered a relapse, for the tent which had formerly accommodated nineteen was only required for three.

The following night I strolled away from the camp as I had done before the "push". The divisional band was not playing, neither did the boisterous laughter of the sergeants echo across the ground. An atmosphere of tragedy overlay the camp, and well it might, for I had heard, unofficially, that the battalion had sustained three hundred and seventy-five casualties; and I had no reason to doubt the assertion.

THE MENIN ROAD BATTLE

Some of the newspapers named it the battle of the pill-boxes, others the Menin Road battle, and all of them acclaimed it a great British victory. I suppose it was, if measured in the term of square yards gained, but I rather thought that if every unit engaged had fared as disastrously as ours, the victory was purely illusory

CHAPTER XXII

DODGING A WORKING PARTY

JUST a week later the battalion, reinforced by sundry details and a small draft, were again preparing to march to the trenches. Rifles were piled outside the tents, and equipment and Lewis guns lay on the ground in readiness.

Tanky was sitting on his kit looking anything but cheerful. I felt more elated than usual.

"You're a lucky cove," said Tanky.

"I am," I agreed.

That summed up the situation. Tanky was bound for the trenches. I was staying behind.

It came about in this manner.

The sergeant-major had again decided that it was about time I took a stripe. I differed, knowing full well that a lance-corporal is the Cinderella of the battalion and the maid of all work to anyone senior to himself. But the sergeant-major was insistent, pointing out that my experience with the gun should be placed on a proper footing, and he told me to think it over.

I thought it over, and the outcome was, I blossomed forth in orders as a full-blown unpaid lance-corporal, authorized to wear that useful appendage commonly known as "the dog's hind leg".

The actual ceremony of "putting it up", that is, sewing the stripe to the tunic sleeves, took place in the tent amid the rude and caustic comments of half the platoon; but I was able to smile pretty broadly when I found that the first favour it conferred was that of missing the next spell of trenches for the purpose of undergoing a course of instruction.

I did not like the unpaid part of the business. No one would, with the exception of the War Office people, who saved threepence per day by upholding these one-sided promotions; but the great thing to do was to get the second hind leg and thus get paid for the first.

"It's a funny thing," said Tanky, continuing the conversation, "I've never been one of the lucky ones. I got my stripe in England, and there was nothing to miss those days."

"Perhaps you'll be getting another just now," I replied. "How about one rolling up just before the next 'push'."

Tanky did not reply. His eyes were strained beyond the range of the tents

"Good Lord, look what's coming," he cried.

I looked in the direction he was pointing.

"Well, I'll be hanged, it's Shorty!" I exclaimed.

Nothing had been heard of him since the night we left Spoilbank, and no one knew whether he had been killed, wounded, or was officially missing. But here he was, apparently sound in wind and limb, with the same old grin on his face, and a well-filled sandbag on his shoulder.

"What! You ain't brought our rations back, have you," yelled Tanky.

"That's my kit, you chump," answered Shorty, dumping his load on the ground.

"What's doing?" he asked, looking at the piled rifles. "Not the trenches again, surely?"

"Certain," said Tanky laconically.

"Wish I'd had another blasted day then."

"Get hit?" I asked.

"A bit," answered Shorty, rather weakly.

"Only a bit," put in Tanky.

"Enough to get away with," Shorty replied.

He gave us the details. It appeared that before we reached the assembly trenches a shell had burst and he had received a fragment of the shrapnel. He said he felt a slight shock and a burning sensation, and did not wait to investigate how far he was injured, but got quickly away to a dressing-station and then on to the Casualty Clearing Depot, where he was detained for the few days.

"You know how to do it, you do," said Tanky. "You ain't going to put a wound stripe up for that bit, are yer?"

"Win 'em and wear 'em," replied Shorty with a grin.

There was no doubt but that he had received a wound of some kind, or otherwise he would not have been detained at the Clearing Depot. It must have been extremely small, for at subsequent visits to the baths I made a point of looking for the scar, but without success. It went to prove that the bravest of men will not face death if they can find the least excuse to avoid it.

DODGING A WORKING-PARTY

Shorty went away to find out how he was fixed with regard to the trenches, and presently he returned much relieved to know that he was not to be included in that unhappy band.

"You're a lucky cove, you are," said Tanky for the second time.

The companies fell into line and went their weary way, and we fell into line and, headed by the band, marched to Kemmel as though treading on air.

The instruction classes began immediately There was quite a decent crowd of us all told, and we came under the personal supervision of the regimental sergeant-major. He was a typical product of Aldershot, fiery and sarcastic. He meant licking us into shape, and he did.

"Come from behind that rifle," he would yell. "I shan't go off with a crash and a bang."

I was not so sure, for he was the nearest approach to a human whizbang that Nature could devise, and I thought if I did not get shell-shock under him I never should in the line. He persisted in reminding us that we were escaping a spell in the trenches, and if we were not mighty careful he would send us there.

"Bawl, man! Bawl!" he would shriek, during a class devoted to giving orders. "You'll die of starvation when you get back on your newspaper round. That's if you get back, which isn't likely. You don't think the army's going to loose you chaps, do you, after all the money they've spent on you. Don't think it, my lads. Take my tip, when the war's over, what's left of you will get packed off to India, or some other place. Stop that grinning, you on the right; you won't feel like grinning if I return you to duty."

Twelve days we had under this martinet and not a man grumbled. Far better to be bullied and ridiculed by him than stand in filthy trenches to be shot at.

The class ended all too soon, and some time later I resumed acquaintance with that pleasant abode, Spoilbank. It became our reserve billets during a period of trench-work in the neighbouring sectors, and from it we debouched nightly on unpleasant working parties.

"D" Company set out one night with the intention of reporting at an engineer dump to pick up material for the front line. We had traversed the greater part of Oaf trench when we encountered heavy shelling immediately in front. The officer in charge was inclined to be a trifle shaky.

"Back to the dugouts," he cried, and back we ran some hundreds of yards when he reversed the order and called for us to come on again. Exactly the same thing happened, and when for the third time we approached the scene of the shelling and the officer again ordered us back, there was no stopping the men until the safety of Spoilbank was reached. The cry of wolf had been called once too often.

Inside the dugouts we talked over the affair and hoped that we should not be expected to go out again.

"Damned if I'll go," said one.

"They'll have to drag me next time," said another.

"What about it, Tanky?" I asked. "Are you on if they call us out?"

"I've bin once, and I don't move another bloomin' inch," said Tanky vehemently.

"Neither do I; hang the working party," I added.

A few minutes later.

"Fall in the working party," sounded along the passages. Grumbling and cursing, the men filed towards the main roadway. The company officer came on the scene and ordered each man a generous ration of rum. I drank mine and finally decided I would give it a miss, so did Tanky.

We commenced to move down the passage. On each side ran narrow tunnels, some lighted, some in darkness I slipped into one of the dark ones and waited for a few minutes before I emerged.

Then I discovered that several others, including a sergeant, a corporal, and a lance-corporal, had done the same thing. We looked at each other with a certain amount of guiltiness.

"Well, we're all in the same boat. What we've got to do now is to lie low and wait till they come back," said the sergeant.

We lay low for about five hours, and when the party returned we slipped amongst them just as we had slipped out, and nobody was any the wiser. It sounds immoral, this shirking of duty, but war is immoral and we were products of the war. "Swinging the lead" was a common pastime. Everybody swung it when they could. A man who could successfully fool the Medical Officer and get away from the horror did so, but usually the Medical Officer could not be fooled. Dodging fatigues, working parties, and anything uncongenial was fair game, and was played to the full. Number one, first, second, and last was the maxim, and often it meant the difference between a live body and a rotting corpse.

CHAPTER XXIII

ABOUT POSTS AND WIRING

DURING a wet spell we moved into a sector which almost beggars description. It was unnaturally dark when we reached the position and there were no trenches. The companies were split up amongst the many pill-boxes which the enemy had been forced to leave behind. They afforded unique protection, for the walls were built of solid concrete capable of withstanding many direct hits. As usual, Lewis gunners were required for post duty well in advance of the main body.

The ground was a quagmire and literally covered with shell-holes, and there was no beaten track to follow. From the post I was to occupy, to a pill-box which housed the platoon, ran a wire, supported at intervals by stakes driven into the ground. We had to hold the wire at the commencement, and letting it slip through our fingers, go where it led us. Through shell-holes and swamps we waded, irrespective of the depth of the water, never daring to loose the wire for fear of becoming lost. Step by step we trudged through the mud and at length reached the post. It was little more than a hole and for three days and three nights we occupied it without relief. There was not a sufficient number of men to provide reliefs, we were told.

During daylight, beyond the reach of help if it was needed, we passed hours of misery, alone, yet not alone, for occasionally would come the whir of aircraft engines, and a machine bearing the familiar red, white, and blue rings of the Royal Air Force would pass overhead, bringing that comforting feeling of comradeship: that friends could see our plight. We sat on heaps of muddy earth, cold, wet, and always hungry, talking little, but thinking many things.

On the second night, just as it had become dark, I saw the shadowy figures of several men creep up to within thirty or forty yards of the post—Germans taking up their night positions.

When the visiting officer came round I rather foolishly reported the occurrence.

"Did you fire on them?" asked the officer.

"No, sir," I replied.

"Why didn't you, then?"

"Because of disclosing the position of the post."

"Oh, never mind that; if you see them going out in the morning, let them have a drum."

The officer went back to the pill-box.

"Cheeky devil," said one of the gunners, "he must think we're barmy."

The position reminded me of one of those "What would you do?" competitions so popular some years before. Here was a British Lewis gun post. A few yards away a German machine-gun. He might know that I was here. He might not. The odds were in favour of him knowing. I could kill him as he was coming in, or when he was going out, just as I preferred, but the simple fact that he was there greatly enhanced my security. Without him I should be a helpless target for the German batteries, and if I do kill him, or even attempt to, the enemy gunners will have many hours of daylight to exact revenge. The crux of the situation was that theirs was a night post only, mine day and night. By firing indiscreetly I should not assist the British cause one iota, but I should certainly assist some of us along the speedy road to eternity.

"Seen anything more of the Germans?" asked the officer on his next visit.

"No, sir," I lied, "they must have crawled out and back."

This irregular development of trench warfare, which was akin to fraternizing, was practised to a greater degree than the higher commands imagined. It was the continuation of the policy of you leave me alone and I will leave you alone. On some sectors it was more pronounced than others. Neither plan nor previous arrangement was responsible for its adoption. Just plain common sense and the desire to live.

I have relieved posts where the enemy could not fail to see us. We have stood there fully exposed while the men we had come to relieve climbed out of the trench. They have scuttled hastily to the rear and we have settled in their places, and then the enemy has signalled his presence by opening fire. All men are human and soldiers are only men.

Caught up in the vortex of war by patriotism, love of adventure, or a military service act, man quickly finds himself endeavouring to survive the condition created by man. Seated in a comfortable arm-chair by a glowing fire, the civilian can easily feel patriotic as he reads of some glorious feat of arms, or when he hears the stirring music of a passing band, but to the man marooned on a lonely outpost patriotism sheds its glamour. "Who dies if England lives" is a phrase inspired, but different circumstances produce different results, and "I live if England dies" might sometimes appropriately be substituted. I never heard the refrain of "*Deutschland Uber Alles*" float from the German lines, nor heard "God Save the King" sung in ours.

Patriotism is another word which is so elastic. People were patriotic for lending their money at five and a half per cent, and industrial chiefs were patriotic for producing shells at exorbitant prices. We all like to be patriotic in our own way.

. . . . .

We occupied another uncongenial post a few days later. It was situated further to the right and a long weary march was necessary before we reached the final trench. This particular trench was not a front line in the accepted sense, because it was not aligned on the actual front and had been dug chiefly to connect up the various pill-boxes which formed the sleeping quarters for men off duty. Beyond the posting of an occasional sentry, there was no attempt to man this trench in the usual way.

Prior to leaving the reserve quarters we had been split up into posts and duly numbered. Mine was number five, and close to one of the pill-boxes I picked up the guide who was to take us out. The ground was in the usual sticky condition associated with wet weather, and already wearied by the inward march we rapidly approached a distressing state of exhaustion.

Two of us were carrying the gun alternately, and my helpmate had just taken it from me when he slipped into a deep shell-hole and crawled out minus the gun. This was a terrible disaster, and some minutes had elapsed before we finally dragged it out, saturated and muddy.

The post was still a considerable distance, and the exhaustion increased to such an extent that when a man fell he crawled on hands and knees until he could regain sufficient breath to stand. We reached the position in a condition of utter helplessness. The trench was deep in water, which reached above the knees, but glad to have got there we stood in it panting like worn-out dogs.

The next step was to attend to the gun. I stripped it on the muddy parapet in total darkness, and after carefully drying and oiling each part, reassembled it. Then I walked some distance from the post and tried it and found it had suffered no ill-effects.

The post had been dug on the extreme edge of a German cemetery, which covered about an acre, and I thought at first that the site had been selected to secure immunity from shell-fire, but I was to suffer speedy disillusionment.

On the left of the post was a line of twisted willows which ran directly to the German positions, and this was a source of continued anxiety because of the ready means it offered for the incursion of enemy patrols, bent on killing. We obviated this by posting a sentry during the hours of darkness.

Shorty held a post a couple of hundred yards to the left and Tanky was somewhere on the other side of the cemetery. It was an astounding fact that the line was being held by a mere handful of men, between whom was sufficient space for the passage of innumerable enemy patrols. I often wondered what would happen if a couple of posts were wiped out and the enemy assaulted the line. He would have a clear course to the trench which held the main body, and in my humble opinion they would have been totally insufficient to withstand any sustained attack. However, to the ordinary man in the line little is known of the actual deposition of troops in the neighbourhood, and the probability was that such contingencies were adequately provided for.

During the long hours of the night I made a practice of strolling along to Shorty's post, and he would pay a return visit in due course On one of these occasions he was seated on a box of ammunition at the end of the trench which held the least water, and over which some previous occupant had placed a sheet of iron. Just as the visiting officer was coming I heard a frightful snore. I shook him violently, but could not stop him snoring, for he was one of those peculiar unfortunates who rarely fall asleep but lapse into unconsciousness. It would not do for Shorty to be found asleep on outpost duty, so I got one of the gunners to bring him round while I engaged the officer in conversation some distance away. Ultimately Shorty was roused from his state of coma and was able to present a dignified appearance at the correct moment.

ABOUT POSTS AND WIRING

During our occupation of this post the company officer decided that we must be protected by wiring the front. Those before us had done without wire and I wanted to do the same, but no argument is allowed with superior officers, and the wiring party came up.

They could not have realized that they were so close to the Germans, for they tramped about No Man's Land as though it was a village green. They talked and laughed and made a general uproar, so it seemed to me, and when they had finished, our once insignificant position was half-surrounded with a network of stakes and barbed wire. The next morning the enemy showed his disapproval by attempting to blow it down. He succeeded to some extent, but during the process our nerves suffered badly, and so did the little wooden crosses which fringed the post.

Wiring as a general rule is a nasty job, and if the enemy is near enough, an extremely dangerous task. We were enjoying twenty-four hours' "rest" in the trench behind, when I was picked to go with a wiring party. Having reached the selected position I was given a rifle and sent twenty yards in front to cover the working party. After an hour of waiting and watching, I saw two figures coming apparently from the German lines. I held the rifle at the ready and glanced behind me to find that I had been wired out. Visions of a concentration camp flashed through my mind. I challenged, but still they came quietly on. Again I shouted, and was in the act of taking the first pressure when I recognized the voice of the captain.

"My God, sir," I said. "I almost shot you."

"It's a good job you didn't," he replied, with a laugh.

It appears that they had been patrolling the front and had taken a course which brought them to a different point than was intended.

A similar experience once befell me whilst engaged on a wiring job. I was occupying a post which was devoid of wire, and we received instructions to tackle the work ourselves. Wire and stakes were sent up and we proceeded some distance in front and commenced twisting in the spiral stakes. It was darker than usual and quite impossible to see a yard ahead. We planted out four or five stakes at intervals and then could not find the rolls of wire. When, after a prolonged search, we found the wire, we had lost the stakes. While looking for the stakes we heard voices which were not English, so we retired to a safer position.

We started again by driving in a stake and securing the wire to it immediately, then a few yards away another stake, and so on until we had made a tolerably good job of it. Then we decided to return, but we had walked round ourselves so many times that we were not altogether sure which was the right way back. I suggested one way, another fellow suggested the opposite, so we compromised by waiting until the Germans fired a star-shell, when we set our course in the reverse direction.

We had walked further than we considered should have been necessary when we heard a familiar sound and flung ourselves to the ground. It was the cocking handle of a Lewis gun being pulled back preparatory to firing. We had unconsciously strayed back to the post of another gun-team.

When morning dawned we looked expectantly for the result of our night's work, and found that we had done the wiring admirably, but, instead of being parallel with the post, it was running diagonally towards the German lines. That wiring had to be repeated the next night.

During the latter stages of our sojourn in Spoilbank and its neighbourhood I was, in army language, "sweating on leave". Providing I could get safely away from these sectors, leave would be certain before I entered any more, and knowing this to be the position, I was rather anxious that nothing should go amiss. The last three days was to be spent in reserve. "D" Company was billeted in a detached portion of the dugouts on the far side of Oaf trench.

On the first night, in pouring rain, I was included in a working party with the task of carrying duckboards to the front line. It was an uncomfortable business, and when we returned, so dark was it that we were quite unable to find the entrance to the dugouts. The whole of the remainder of the night was spent in groping aimlessly about, and it was not until morning came that we were able to locate them.

A few minutes before the expected relief was due the enemy commenced a bombardment of the dug-outs. Sitting in the passages, the crashing of the shells above filled us with dismay. I thought of my imminent leave and could have wrung my hands to realize I had yet to take a chance before it could materialize.

"Reliefs coming," rose the cry.

I went to the entrance and saw them in the distance, and also saw and heard the bursting of the heavies around the dugouts. Before the relief could come in we should have to clear out, because in this part there was not sufficient room to accommodate more than a company.

"Get ready to move," came the order, and we dressed and crowded towards the opening. The "carry on" order followed very quickly. We ran and ducked. We lay on the ground time after time. Oaf trench was a jungle of wreckage and hindered our flight, but we safely reached the duckboards leading to Spoilbank proper.

They were being shelled, but it was now or never, and without pausing for breath we cleared that quarter of a mile in record time, and a few minutes later were walking down the main passage which brought us to a position of comfortable security.

CHAPTER XXIV

CHRISTMAS IN THE TRENCHES

NEW STREET STATION, BIRMINGHAM, during war-time, was the scene of many joyful reunions, and many, many tearful partings. Of all the trains which steamed away from the Midland city in the latter part of 1917, none was better known or better hated than the 12.35 a.m. to London. It was an obliging train, always waiting for you when you stepped on the platform. Its pedigree was of the finest. No unversed recruits desecrated its stuffy compartments. Hard-bitten trench-grimed veterans rubbed shoulders with airmen who had won their wings, and sailors who knew what it was to feel the presence of death. One and all knew the ropes and realized fully what lay at the journey's end.

Standing by the open door of a compartment might be seen a sad-faced woman, trying hard to look cheerful.

"Never mind, Joe, the war will soon be over now," she says bravely to her khaki-clad man who is biting his lip to restrain his emotion.

"That's right, old girl," he replies. "Another three months will do it, and then no more partings for us."

They don't mean it. They know quite well that

the war may last for years, and that possibly this is their last farewell, but they like to part in this manner.

A man with a flattened nose who had enjoyed many one's over the eight is voicing his opinion, for all and sundry to hear.

"I've had nine months out there. It's bloody hell, that's what it is. Nine months, I tell yer, in the trenches, not base wallering. Christ help me if I've got ter do another nine months."

Yes, the 12.35 was a dreadful train. It carried away hosts of men never to return. It was a mechanical tumbril which never failed to deliver the goods. Its punctuality was disgusting. Promptly to the minute the guard would hold aloft his green lantern, the engine would emit a shrill whistle, and to the accompaniment of slamming doors and weeping women the 12.35 would glide into the tunnel.

Two glorious weeks of civilization and freedom from shell-fire. What a time it had been. How I had revelled in the wonderful comfort of home life. How I had marvelled at the placid demeanour of everyone.

Kind elderly ladies had asked me if I had killed many Germans, and when I said I did not know, they were disappointed. They seemed to think the killing of Germans was something commonplace, like swatting flies.

The trouble was that England had become reconciled to war and the casualty lists, and the mourning which was horribly fashionable. I left England firmly convinced that I should not return again unless on a stretcher. I should have made a will had my worldly goods been sufficient to warrant it, but they were not. I did not think it possible that an infantryman directly exposed to the perils of attack and defence could escape indefinitely, and my reasoning was sound. Multitudes had died with smaller war records than mine, and the hospitals were crowded with men who never knew the mud slopes of the Ancre. I calculated that I had three chances, and only three. Getting wounded, taken prisoner, or being killed. The possibility of carrying on throughout the war was too remote to contemplate. Previously I had lived and hoped for leave, and now that had come and gone I was without hope, excepting—down in my heart I nursed a secret feeling that I would welcome an enemy bullet, or a piece of shrapnel, but I wanted to have the choice. In the arm or leg would not matter so much if only it was moderate, but not the head, or anywhere which might produce after-effects.

I was sick to the death with the agony of the life I was forced to lead. I wanted to get both legs out of the grave, to leave the horror behind and say never again. Never again would I become enthused over newspaper stunts and recruiting propaganda. To hell with war was my sentiment, and to hell with the war lords. I was not alone in my sentiment. I knew the Tommies of the trenches and the posts better than did the gushy writers in some weekly periodicals. "No peace until Germany is crushed," they cried, and Tommy in the outpost of the wilderness, with tortured mind and lice-infested body, with dead men lying within his vision, and death lurking ever near, would cry from the depth of his soul, "Give us peace, lest I die also."

When I arrived at Calais I learned that something had happened which was very much my concern. As a result of the German coup the division had been hurried to the Cambrai front. I had read of the attack in the newspapers, and I had little imagined that I should be sent so quickly to the scene of those unpleasant incidents.

It required six days of travelling, with much interrogating of R.T.O.'s, and living the life of a nomad before I eventually tracked down the Worcesters in the village of Neuville. The battalion was in the line, but a host of men including sergeant-majors, bandsmen, and other details, were apparently enjoying a fairly tolerable time. It was the 21st of December, and I had been anticipating Christmas under congenial circumstances, but within an hour of reporting myself for duty I was warned to prepare for the trenches the next day. Accordingly, after a night's sleep and a casual look round, I accompanied the ration limbers along an unfamiliar road which led past Havrincourt wood, and through Metz, to Ribecourt. The villages in this part of the country were in ruins, not as a result of shell-fire, but systematically destroyed during the enemy evacuation in the early part of the year.

Near Ribecourt was the communication trench, and a comparatively short journey brought me to the support line. Another man who had returned from leave had come with me from the Neuville camp, and we were on the point of reporting to the company officer that we had returned to duty when a stray bullet pierced the side of his neck, and without the least sign of excitement or emotion, he said,

"So long, I'm off," and was gone before I was able to fully realize what had happened.

It speedily convinced me that the place was unhealthy, and after I had reported I made a point of inquiring as to the danger spots of the trench.

I found Shorty and Tanky adapting themselves to the new conditions with the stolidity born of experience. Tanky had just received one of his wonderful parcels from home, and a small bottle of whisky was in his hand when I discovered him.

"Welcome home, here's the best," he said, tipping up the bottle with his head well back.

"If this is the best you can offer I don't think much of it," I replied.

"Mate, that's Black and White," said Tanky, when he had uncoupled his mouth.

"I mean the trenches, not what you've got there," said I.

"Oh, you always feel like that when you first get back," put in Shorty. "You sort of get rusty when you're away from the 'doings', but you'll feel quite all right again when he's dropped a few 'five-nines' round you."

"Much shelling then?" I inquired.

"Enough to go on with," he answered.

"Now don't get putting the wind up him," said Tanky.

"It ain't half so bad 'ere as we have had it. Just a few before breakfast and not much after. It's the machine-guns that's doing we the damage. He snipes with the blarsted things."

"And the frosts," said Shorty. "Damned cold frosts too, and no dugouts to pop into occasionally.

There's only one perishin' dugout in this trench, and, of course, they've made that company headquarters."

Among other things, I learned that there were no posts but there was a rigid system of standing-to from dusk until dawn. It was feared that the enemy might attempt to repeat his coup of a short time ago, and no chances were being taken.

Presently I joined the gun-team and commenced the routine of keeping watch. As the night advanced and the wind became keener, I fairly shivered with the cold. Cap comforters, a species of overgrown night-cap, which had formerly been so useful for protecting the ears on cold nights, were barred. It had been discovered that they deadened the hearing, and so it was necessary to face the icy blasts without protection of any kind. There is nothing more trying than looking over the top of a trench into outer darkness, hour after hour, with nothing to break the monotony, and at that time of the year the night was of fifteen hours' duration. So intense was the cold that to prevent the oil on the gun from freezing, it was essential to fire a few rounds occasionally, and much of the machine-gun fire which was prevalent could be attributed to that reason.

When the rations came early in the morning I had rather a shock. In this instance they were issued by the platoon sergeant, assisted by a full corporal, and one loaf between six was all we got. The remainder of the rations was correspondingly reduced.

"How long has this been going on?" I asked of one of the gunners.

"Ever since we got down here," he replied. "It

was eight in a loaf yesterday. How the devil they expect chaps to keep well on such grub I don't know."

"Why, it isn't a decent meal," I said.

"I've written home for some grub;" he answered.

"Good Lord", I thought. "Writing home for grub and they expect us to win the war."

It began to snow, lightly at first, but rapidly increased to such an extent that in a few hours the ground was covered to a depth of several inches.

On Christmas Eve we moved to another part of the trench. Near where we posted the gun was a small funkhole in the trench, and we took turns to have a smoke and a rest from the cutting wind. Some rice came up in the rations which, on the whole, were no better than the previous issues. We boiled the rice in melted snow and ate it with relish. Then the mail came along, and aided by the light of a full moon we read cards from home, wishing us a merry Christmas. Just on the turn of midnight the Germans forwarded their greetings. They exploded with dull thuds which we again mistook for dud shells, although we should have known better. It was some time before I could adjust my respirator, because I had swallowed a fair amount of mustard gas and was busily employed in trying to sneeze my head off. Directly after "stand down" the company officer presented each of us with two packets of "Players", and wished us the compliments of the season.

I was not feeling so well as I should like to, and did not know whether to attribute the feeling to the boiled rice or the mustard gas.

While I was debating this important point a staff officer with red tabs came rushing round the trench.

Previously the captain had ordered the gun to be mounted for anti-aircraft work during the daytime, but there was no aeroplanes about and not likely to be any, so after adjusting it in the required position we had retired to the funkhole and settled down.

The staff officer looked first at the gun, then at us.

"Who is in charge here?" he asked, somewhat haughtily.

I stood up to attention.

"I am, sir."

"Oh you—well, where is the aircraft sentry?"

"No aeroplanes about, sir."

"Never mind that, the sentry should be posted. I'll report this neglect of duty to Headquarters. 'Pon my word, not a man near the gun."

He strode away.

"Why, the damned idiot," said a gunner. "It was only a pet idea of the captain's and ain't at all necessary."

A few minutes later the captain came round.

"Staff officer been here?" he asked, pleasantly.

I mentioned what had happened, and he chuckled.

"Quite all right," he said. "He mistook this for the front line. You can pull the gun down. I don't think it will serve any useful purpose there."

On the afternoon the symptoms of sickness had developed to such an extent that I decided to take an extreme step. I sought the captain and told him what was the matter.

"I want a special sick report made out, sir."

He was astounded.

"You understand that it is a very serious matter

to put in a special sick report in the trenches," he said.

"I understand," I replied.

"It will be a sure court-martial if you get duty," he continued, gravely.

"I shan't get duty. I want treatment, that's very evident," I answered. He made out the sick report and detailed a stretcher-bearer to accompany me to the first-aid station. I vomited most of the way, and when I arrived at the station my temperature was immediately taken.

"One hundred point five," said the assistant to the Medical Officer.

"Take that bed in the corner and see what a night's sleep will do," said the M.O.

I was given medicine and passed a fairly good night, and the next morning my temperature was again taken.

"Ninety-nine point eight," said the assistant.

"What is your duty?" asked the M.O.

"Lewis gunner," I replied.

He looked at the thermometer again.

"They are very short of Lewis gunners," he said. "I think you had better go back to your company and if you become any worse, report here again."

And so I went back to the company and rapidly became better.

During the few hours I had been away they had moved into the front line. It began to snow again and the wind, getting up strongly, a pretty bad blizzard was soon raging. A section of the trench was terribly exposed and it became necessary to change the men very frequently. I dreaded my turn in the exposed position, for there was no proper trench. It was little better than a ridge with nothing at the back to protect us from the biting wind and the snow which blew and piled up against our legs. Hour succeeded hour and still the blizzard raged, and it was so cold that we were obliged to continually stamp our feet to restore the circulation. The desire to sleep was overwhelming but had to be shaken off, for men can die of exposure if they relax movement of the body under such conditions.

The following night I was warned for a battle patrol. Half a dozen men were required to enter the German lines and seek a prisoner for identification purposes, and two of us with the gun were wanted as a covering party. White smocks were in readiness and also white covers for steel hats and rifles. Rigged out in these, we looked a picturesque assembly. Shorty, like an overgrown umpire at a cricket match, thought we were on a good thing.

"Jerry will take us for a pierrot troupe," he said.

"Or ready-made corpses with the shrouds on," said Tanky.

A ravine ran from the front line directly to the enemy position, and our instructions were to follow the ravine until we came within sight of the Germans. Then we were to make the best of any opportunity to capture one.

With a second-lieutenant in command we crept cautiously through the wire. As covering party, our position was at the rear so that if anything untoward occurred the others could make good their escape under the protection of the gun.

It was an eerie task, this creeping towards the

unknown. We kept to the right-hand bank as the least likely place we should encounter machine-gun fire. A few trees here and there gave excellent cover, and the white smocks matched the snow so perfectly that there was little possibility of being seen at a distance. A hundred yards and we could hear the sounds of a German working party repairing the trench. Then voices, which was thrilling but not pleasant. A little further along and a solitary figure was seen. A sentry on duty. We lay in the snow and watched him walking backwards and forwards to keep warm. His rifle was slung over his shoulder, and his hands were encased in big gloves. He was walking a matter of twenty paces in each direction and the trodden path was clearly outlined. The officer whispered to me to remain where I was while they crept within his beat.

Step by step, they crept along until they had reached a position which would bring the man directly into their arms, but even as he turned to come in their direction, someone whose excitement overcame his discretion cried:

"Shoot the swine."

Uttering a startled cry the man leaped to the side and disappeared down a dugout.

It would have been suicidal to attempt an attack on the dugout, for we knew not the location of the enemy troops, and the officer did not hesitate.

"Come on, boys. Back as quickly as you can."

They ran past me and a few seconds later I picked up the gun and followed. A fusillade of rifle fire poured down the ravine, but fortunately we had kept to the slope and were unharmed. In response, I fired off the magazine which was on the gun, and then made no bones about getting back to the trench as speedily as possible. It was an inglorious exploit, but it ended happily, inasmuch that no one was injured, and we were grateful for the double issue of rum that was issued by order of the captain.

Soon afterwards we were relieved from this position and in another blinding snowstorm groped our way to the reserve trench. Dugouts were scarce, but we were fortunate enough to find a funkhole capable of housing the gun-team, and with an old blanket secured to the outside we were protected from the icy blasts which blew along the trench, otherwise the funkhole was a filthy abode, with water trickling from above as the heat of our bodies warmed the atmosphere.

The scarcity of food was becoming something more than a thing of the moment. We were living in a constant state of gnawing hunger, for the day's issue was insufficient for more than one substantial meal. I adopted the plan of dividing my supply into portions, with the resolve that I would eat each portion only at its appointed time, and the plan might have worked admirably had I been alone, but the mere sight of others digging into a tin of bully, or sucking a piece of cold fat bacon, was enough to upset any plan that could be evolved; and usually about midday my next meal was down at the transport lines being packed into sandbags for the evening ration party.

Discontent was rife. The troops knew they were not getting the quantity as authorized by army regulations. The official minimum was a pound of bread per day, and not at the best of times did we enjoy such a generous allowance, excepting when casualties made such inevitable, and now that it had dwindled to a regular slice per day it simply added to the torture of the privations which we were forced to endure.

While out of the line it was always possible to augment a scanty issue by purchasing chocolate and biscuits, but in the trenches there was only the bare ration to depend on, and any diminution of that ration meant ultimately a diminution of efficiency.

"Can't understand it," growled Shorty, on one occasion, "the further you are from the line the more grub you get. It's half a loaf a man at the base, and it oughter be half a loaf here if we had our rights, but there's too many fingers in the pie before it reaches us. Everybody who handles it has a pickin', blarst 'em, and us poor devils can stew in our own juice."

"And no one seems to care a damn whether we stew or freeze," I replied.

"'Taint the officers' fault," continued Shorty. "Every day they ask quarters what the rations are like, and when he tells 'em rotten they say it oughter be better than it is, and that's about as far as they can get."

"And it isn't quarters's fault," I said. "He couldn't eat the difference if he tried. It's either thundering bad management or a twist on somewhere."

Sometimes, to supplement the bread issue, a certain quantity of oatmeal would be sent up to the trenches, and this, boiled in water with a little sugar added, went under the name of "bergoo". It was hardly better than weak skilly, but welcome nevertheless.

For some days there had been no oatmeal, and I had a fairly strong suspicion that we were being robbed under our very noses.

The platoon sergeant and a corporal would receive the rations for the platoon, and take them down a dugout for the purpose of dividing them into sections.

One day I was talking to the sergeant and noticed something on his leather jerkin.

I touched it with my fingers.

"Bergoo," I said. "So some did come up in the rations, after all."

"Only a bit, not enough to divide," answered the sergeant.

"Damn that for a tale," I replied. "I want sufficient for six men, or somebody's going to know of this."

I fetched a mess-tin.

"I'm coming for that 'bergoo'," I said.

He rather ungraciously took the mess-tin from me and went down the dugout, presently returning with it filled to the brim.

"I shouldn't tell the others because we've got no more left," he said.

I took that canteen of oatmeal and showed it to every man in the platoon, at the same time advising them to get after their share, and they stormed the dugout and cursed the sergeant, but for once he had told the truth. There was no more left.

This pilfering of the rations by dishonest N.C.O.'s was not an uncommon occurrence and usually happened when food was scarce, for it was then that they could not resist the temptation to help themselves.

Towards the end of the month, the Germans

bombarded the line on the right of our position, and the extreme limit of the shelling caught the trench and inflicted several casualties. We heard later that he had attempted a raid but had been repulsed, and the night following the occurrence we had orders to relieve the unit affected. This necessitated a fairly long jaunt through the trenches, which were treacherous with the accumulation of frozen snow and ice.

I went straight into a post, where I remained for New Year's Day. We found the line fairly quiet again, but the cold was such that our fingers and toes became painfully swollen. A wide expanse of perfectly flat country was within our view, with Cambrai showing plainly in the distance, and we were astounded and not a little interested to see an occasional train puffing along some miles behind the German lines.

The front line was better than usual and was liberally supplied with dugouts. I was sitting on the steps of a dugout after being relieved from the post when along came an officer wearing his respirator.

He looked at me and then pushed up the bottom part so that he could speak.

"Why have you taken off your respirator?" he demanded.

"I have had no orders to put it on," I replied.

"Then put it on immediately. The gas alarm was given an hour ago," he said.

I was amazed, but adjusted the respirator, and when the officer had gone I went a few more steps down the dugout and took it off again, for I was quite sure that the suspected gas was mist, otherwise I should have been suffering badly from the effects of it.

With an increasing number of men going home

on leave, and a larger amount of sickness than usual, the strength of the battalion was considerably reduced. Consequently, much extra work fell to us. The posts were manned at times by scratch teams, three parts of whom knew nothing whatever of the manipulation of the Lewis gun, but this impossible state of affairs was rectified by the arrival of a large draft.

I was sorry for that draft, for it included many boys who had been called up under the Military Service Act. Direct from the base camps, they were pitchforked into the front line without any preliminary hardening-off, or opportunity of previously making the acquaintance of the men with whom they were to live and die. Small wonder that for some time they were quite unable to adapt themselves to standing in freezing trenches, or of coping with the hundred and one jobs which were a feature of trench life.

Soon after the arrival of the draft I came across Shorty and Tanky. It was not often that we were together in the front line, for usually one or the other would be occupying an advanced post.

We indulged in a heated argument about the policy of introducing boys of nineteen years of age into the trenches, and from this question of the moment the conversation had drifted to that well-worn topic, conscientious objectors.

Shorty was at first emphatic in his opinion that they should be brought out at the point of the bayonet and forced to take their share of holding the line.

Tanky was not quite so severe, but he thought they should be interned until the war was over.

I was, to a certain extent, holding sides with them because I had a deep-rooted feeling that I should be a conscientious objector in the next war, providing I could get safely out of this.

"It's all very well objecting to war, but it's a whole skin that the blighter's are after keeping," said Shorty.

"Well, even that's natural, isn't it?" I replied.

"It ain't," went on Shorty. "Why should they get off scot-free when the likes of you and me have got to stick this lot, whether we like it or not? How would I stand if I said I didn't believe in any more war and cleared out without getting permission. I'd be stuck up against the wall and shot."

"And you'd deserve to be for bein' such a chunk," put in Tanky.

That remark seemed to take the sting out of Shorty's debating power.

"We should all be conscientious objectors if we could get the chance," I remarked.

"No fear," said Shorty.

"No bloomin' fear," said Tanky.

"How about if we were going over the top in the morning, and they told us that those who didn't believe in going over could stop here and watch the others?" I said.

There was no response.

"Should you go?" I urged.

"No fear," said Shorty.

"No bloomin' fear," said Tanky. "Nor nobody else would. We'd all be standing here looking on."

"That's if Jerry didn't put a barrage on the trench," corrected Shorty.

"And what would happen if they told us that

anybody who didn't believe in war could go back home?" I asked.

"War would be over to-morrow," said Shorty.

"To-night," corrected Tanky.

"So it looks like this," I continued. "The conscientious objectors don't believe in war, and they are keeping out of it, and we don't believe in war and we're here in it."

"We must be blarsted idiots," said Shorty.

"We are," said Tanky.

And that concluded an interesting argument.

CHAPTER XXV

A SCREAM IN THE NIGHT

TOWARDS the end of the first week in January I had a wonderful piece of luck in the form of a notification from battalion headquarters that I was to proceed immediately to the transport lines preparatory to going to a Corps school for a course of Lewis gunnery.

I lost no time in getting away from that atmosphere, and for two weeks enjoyed all the pleasure and safety that a comfortable military school can offer. The food was excellent and bountiful, and contrasted strangely with the amount the troops were receiving in the trenches.

The battalion was billeted in Havrincourt wood when I rejoined. This enormous wood, which covered very many acres, was found distinctly useful for the concentration of troops, and in many places the trees had been felled to allow for the placing of big guns which were able to operate with a minimum chance of detection.

The troops were in a good mood, for an increased scale of payment had just been announced. The news was especially cheerful to myself, because hitherto I had suffered much from that mysterious complaint, "being in debt". However, the new pay being retrospective I discovered that my debts were amply covered, and in addition I had suddenly burst forth as a creditor of the War Office.

Three days later, with Lewis guns and magazine carriers slung on mules, we marched to the Hindenburg line. In various places this wide chalky trench was the communication trench to the advanced lines. In others it was the actual front trench. Its depth surprised us and so did the number of dugouts which were spaced out at intervals of a few yards.

We came to a land of knocked-out tanks, dozens of them spread over a comparatively small area, and to reach a certain post it was necessary to walk between two, no further apart than the houses in an ordinary street. The Germans made a point of shelling these derelict tanks and we never lingered in their vicinity. The snow had cleared, and the weather was milder, but the ground was soft and waterlogged.

When we had completed five days in the posts we came back to reserve, and with the gun-team I was sent on anti-aircraft duty to a field battery. We were accommodated in a covered trench some distance in front of the battery, and until that date I never realized how terrible was the lot of the artillery. Sometimes, for hours on end, enemy shells would pour over the trench to burst near or among the guns, and although cover was available, it could not always be taken advantage of, for if the distress signal was received from the line, or if retaliation was urgently called for, the gunners were compelled to face the shelling and serve their own guns.

Several enemy scouts came over the position, but they kept a good height, and although we were using specially constructed sights, and fired many drums of ammunition, our efforts were of no avail.

I once attended a lecture given by an air force pilot who stressed the importance of machine-gun fire in aerial defence. In his opinion, machine-gun fire from the ground rarely succeeded in destroying a plane, but it presented such a problem of uncertainty to the hostile pilot, with such possibilities as burst petrol tanks and other serious results, that he was ever-ready to give them a wide berth.

After four days with the battery we rejoined "D" Company, and immediately took over another outpost. The line had become more lively and that same night we were subjected to a severe strafe by trench-mortars and whizbangs. The Germans were not holding similar posts and thus were able to strafe us unhindered. Soon after midnight the shelling subsided and was succeeded by a period of intense quietness. Star-shells were absent and we were surrounded by inky blackness. Experience told us that something was amiss, and the whole of the gun-team kept a sharp look-out. Suddenly there arose a piercing scream and then silence again. It set our nerves on edge, but we could do nothing, only wait and watch. Slowly the hours passed by and then from the direction of the front line came creeping figures. Rifles covered them while I cautiously challenged.

"All right, all right," came the voice of an officer I knew. "Has anything happened here?"

"Not here," I replied. "But we have heard a scream over there."

I pointed out the direction.

"Yes, the Germans have taken that post," the

officer answered. "Keep on your guard and watch your rear."

But nothing more was heard that night. Later, when we were back in the front line, the truth of the scream and its result was general knowledge.

It appears that on our right was a bombing post in the charge of a sergeant. A German raiding party had suddenly appeared and rushed the post. Before the enemy reached them, however, the sergeant made good his escape and reported that the post had been captured. A reconnaissance of the position was made and the extraordinary fact revealed that although two men were wounded and one had been killed, the others were doggedly holding the position. The sergeant was immediately sent away from the trenches under escort, and not long afterwards, in the middle of a square formed by the four companies of the battalion, the sentence imposed by a field court-martial was read.

It was, reduced to the ranks and five years imprisonment. The degradation of the stripping of the stalwart sergeant followed and was not nice to look upon.

Discipline is discipline and must be maintained. The instinct of self-preservation is sternly repressed and the man who obeys, under certain circumstances, those original instincts must be punished. Cowardice is the term by which such things are known. To hesitate to advance on machine-gun-infested strongholds is cowardice. A throbbing heart and a harassed mind cries "stay", but unless calm resignation gains unwilling mastery, the verdict is cowardice. And calm resignation is so often confused with bravery.

"Those brave men holding the trenches," people

would say. Rather should it be said that those men were holding the trenches with calm resignation and acceptance of the inevitable. Bravery is spontaneous and is born of the power to subdue the nerves at the critical moment. All men cannot be brave, but most of us can become calmly resigned.

How different is the punishment inflicted on the higher officers who may err. False judgements and reckless commands have made cemeteries where cornfields flourished, and the greatest punishment for the grossest negligence is to be relieved of a command and, perhaps, be given another.

A good General can sacrifice a thousand lives with little to show for it, and the worst that may be said is that, "He wastes men, but he will get his objectives." Insignificant bits of ground are drenched in blood, again and again, to prove nothing more than that our *morale* over the enemy is sustained—and the man who falters during the process can be charged with cowardice. Such is war.

We were lolling about the trench waiting for the expected relief. For over twenty-four hours it had rained incessantly, and we were dejected and morose. A ration of rum was served out and the change in the demeanour of the troops was remarkable. They talked and laughed and were even content.

The relief was hours late coming in, for they had been lost in the labyrinth of trenches. Then commenced an exhausting march. Weary from lack of sleep and unable to see a yard ahead through the driving rain, we dragged ourselves through mud and water, sometimes falling and recovering, sometimes falling and remaining until the hard breathing became normal.

We were taking a different direction, and after covering five miles with slow and painful progress, we came to a light railway. Here was a diminutive engine, and we gladly clambered into the trucks which were attached.

When daylight came, our little engine was puffing its way through open and desolate country, and behind it were the trucks laden with heaps of mud, each heap a man, some standing, some sitting, and the majority fast asleep. We careered noisily into a siding. Transport wagons and limbers were ready to carry equipment and guns.

The band was there, had been waiting several hours. They tuned up. The troops did likewise, and off we went on the last three miles with easy steps and singing hearts.

CHAPTER XXVI

THE GERMAN OFFENSIVE

BARASTE was the mournful remains of a once-thriving village some few kilometres from Bapaume. In March, 1918, the Worcesters were billeted on the outskirts of the village and were undergoing certain training. Big field days were held and mock attacks and counter-attacks were carried out. The villages of Doignies and Hermies on the left of Havrincourt wood were supposed to have fallen to the enemy, and our supposed task was to drive them out. The manœuvres were for the especial benefit of commanders, and the rank and file could make little of the technique of the operations. Then, in the open country surrounding the camp, we trained with tanks, following behind them when they moved, and stopping when they stopped. It all indicated that something big was about to take place, and it was something big as after-events proved.

The Germans were known to be concentrating for a huge assault of the Cambrai-St. Quentin front, and preparations were hastened to counter them. Acres and acres of barbed wire were planted, lines of trenches were dug and many guns brought into position. In woods, and clumps of trees, baby cannon were hiding, with low muzzles, ready to destroy by point-blank fire such enemy tanks which might appear.

That the Germans would attempt to make the coming battle a decisive factor of the war there was no doubt. The entry of America had seriously jeopardized their chances of securing peace by the process of "stalemate", and if they were to make a final bid for victory, the time was now.

The brunt of the assault must fall on the Franco-British armies. The Yanks were coming, but as yet they were a negligible factor on the Western Front, and could not by any chance influence the result, one way or the other.

Day by day, when not otherwise engaged, we marched to various points and assisted with the fortifications, and to me it seemed that no enemy assault could hope to pass such obstacles. It was a foregone conclusion that the Germans would gain initial successes, for the very weight of a massed attack must carry it forward to some extent, and I fervently hoped that it would not be my lot to be holding a post when the attack was launched.

The position of the men in the posts was one of complete hopelessness, and those whose duty it would be to receive the onslaught of the advancing hordes could hope for nothing better than that mercy would be accorded them by the attackers.

What mercy they would receive would largely depend upon their attitude to the enemy, and if they did their duty and resisted to the uttermost, for the ultimate benefit of their comrades behind, then their hope of mercy was small indeed. Outposts in front of the trenches were the sacrifice offered to the enemy, and, providing they functioned long enough for the main body to prepare for action, then the sacrifice was cheap at the price.

In the camp little excitement was manifested. Football matches were played and bouts of boxing staged, and in a quiet corner were a score of men tied to the wheels of limbers. It was part of Field Punishment Number One to be tied to the wheel for an hour a day, and such punishment was meted out for over-staying leave, or some such act of indiscipline. With arms outstretched and feet apart, the delinquents gazed about with bitterness. Some of them whose natures were opposed to discipline of any kind accepted their punishment with contempt, others were degraded and their better natures outraged with the treatment.

The very sight was revolting, more so when it is realized that at any moment these very men may be called upon to give of their best, in the face of untold peril, yet at the same time it cannot be overlooked that rigid discipline is vitally necessary, otherwise a trained unit would quickly degenerate into nothing better than an armed mob.

In the huts sat schools of card-players cheerfully gambling. Pay had just been issued, and five-franc notes had already changed hands in many cases. I joined a pontoon school and handed over my weekly wage in a very short space of time. Shorty was getting his share of running the bank and was doing well. He finished up with sixty francs that once belonged to others, and he invited Tanky and myself to visit the engineers' canteen near Baraste. The canteen stock had run low, but Shorty treated us to some cigarettes and a tin each of unsweetened milk, through which we bored holes and drank the contents. Shorty had now two stripes and was beginning to feel important, but Tanky and I flatly refused to recognize his exalted rank unless compelled to by the presence of a commissioned officer.

We detested calling him "corporal". It didn't sound right even if he liked it on parade.

As Tanky said:

"He was Shorty when I first knew him and he'll be Shorty if he commands the bloomin' battalion."

It was while we were returning from the canteen that Shorty suddenly thought of something.

"Those gun boxes have got to be cleaned, you chaps," he said.

"Then you'll have to come and clean 'em. You don't work that stuff on me," said Tanky.

"Look here, Shorty," I said, "you're suffering from a swelled head since you put that other leg up."

"Don't talk rot," replied Shorty. "I say you've got to clean 'em. I'm responsible for the condition of the gun equipment."

"Then you're the one to do the cleaning," said Tanky, doggedly.

"Well, don't say you haven't been warned," concluded Shorty.

We thought nothing more about it until, on parade next morning, the captain called for the gun boxes to be brought out for inspection and we fetched them, and waited for the crash.

"Did you give orders for the boxes to be cleaned?" asked the captain, of Shorty.

"Yes, sir," replied the latter.

The captain looked us up and down. The four platoon guns were involved.

"I should like to see you four lance-corporals in the orderly room after parade," he said.

An hour or so later we again stood in front of the officer.

"I don't want to have much to say," he began. "I know you are all very great friends of Corporal ——, and that you would not knowingly loose him down, but I want you to remember that he is a full corporal and entitled to the respect of his rank. In future, when he gives you orders, carry them out, and tell him what you think about it afterwards. You may go."

That was all, and outside we found Shorty grinning like a fiendish imp.

"I want you to clean the gun boxes," he said.

And we did.

. . . . .

At dawn, on the 21st of March, we were awakened by a terrific volume of gun-fire. We sat up and looked at each other and then commenced to dress. There was no need for the bugles to blow reveille. The whole camp was awake, for they knew the meaning of that cannonade. It was the tocsin of battle. Germany's hour had struck. Sergeant-majors and sergeants began running here and there after officers who were themselves chasing their superiors for orders, which were inevitable, but lacking.

A near ridge commanded a view of the surrounding country, and from this vantage point we tried to visualize what was happening. A thick mist enveloped the ground, but by the sound we knew that shells were bursting not very far away. A gun of large calibre was firing into a wood behind the camp, the huge shells roaring directly over the huts. Presently, a rapid series of explosions which became greater every minute betokened the fact that a large ammunition dump had been fired.

As the mist slowly lifted, we could see that the whole of the ground extending towards the line was being systematically searched with shell-fire, and the knowledge that we should shortly have to pass through that inferno was not inspiring.

I went back to the hut and burnt all the letters that I was carrying in my pockets. It was a ritual that many men adopted before proceeding to the line. The cooks had joined in the general excitement, and as a consequence served up a cold breakfast of Maconochies, and after that had been disposed of the order was given to stand by.

Meanwhile, in the Battalion Orderly Room sat the operators awaiting orders from Brigade Headquarters Soon after breakfast the companies were paraded in fighting order and then kits were deposited in lines and the men temporarily dismissed.

Packs and blankets were stacked in heaps just as though the camp was being evacuated at an ordinary time, and still we awaited developments.

For several hours we played "spoof" and endeavoured to concentrate our thoughts on anything but what was taking place not so very far away.

Towards midday we paraded again, and the company quartermaster sergeants began to divest themselves of the impedimenta which they had been nursing for many weeks. Bombs, sandbags, Verey lights, and all the essentials for attack or defence, were rapidly distributed.

The roll was called and one or two men detailed to stay behind. How we envied the fortunate ones. Envied the band busy cleaning its instruments and the sergeant-majors who were not coming with us.

"Get dressed."

It was a thrilling experience, this strapping on of equipment for the unknown adventure. Enthusiasm was lacking, but the troops exhibited a spirit of quiet determination.

The first platoon moved away towards the cloud of smoke and fire in the distance.

An hour's march brought us to a wood, a mile from the village of Velu, and here we halted and lay down. News was scanty, but we knew that the front line had fallen with the opening of the attack.

The field kitchens which had accompanied us served up quite a good dinner, and then proceeded back to camp. Soon afterwards a great shell burst in the wood, throwing up a column of earth as high as the trees. Then came others at intervals of a few minutes. Cries of "stretcher-bearers" resounded through the wood. Trees were uprooted wholesale, and the men began to look to the officers for orders to move.

A terrific explosion occurred a few yards from where I was lying, and a fountain of earth poured down on us.

The wood was rapidly becoming untenable, and the men were ordered to file away in sections at fifty yards intervals. It seemed an age before my turn came, but eventually we got away and marched across the open ground to Velu. As far as the eye could see, men were advancing in tiny groups, and shells were bursting with horrible consistence in and among them. A German plane soared above signalling targets, and more than one rifle was fired to lessen his ardour. Through Velu and through the grounds of a ruined château and then on to the open country again. We were now approaching the scene of the rehearsals of a few days ago. Another halt was called and we lay on the ground, exposed to fairly heavy gun-fire. Casualties were becoming numerous and men dug frantically to make cover for themselves. Tanks were seen coming along a valley in our direction. Presently came an order, which astonished every rifleman: "Fix bayonets".

"Why, we're miles behind the blarsted line," said one man.

"I'll bet nobody knows where the line is now," said another.

The tanks reached a position in front of the battalion and commenced to ascend a ridge.

"Advance."

With bayonets fixed, and magazines on the guns, we followed the tanks, but after a time they veered off to the left and we continued alone.

We did not know where we were going, or what had happened since early morning, nor what was likely to happen within the next few hours.

Still another halt. It was getting dark. The shelling had moderated, but bullets were whistling by, and we realized that the enemy could not be far away.

"A" and "B" Companies to the front, and "C" and

"D" in reserve, became the order of progress. Blown-up guns began to appear, and the wreckage of shelters that had housed the gunners was strewn about. Here and there was a khaki-clad corpse gazing upwards with eyes that could not see.

We reached a sunken road. An officer of the 51st Division met us.

"Dig yourselves in," he said, "they will blow this road to hell in the morning."

We rapidly constructed a trench on the sloping bank of the road and prepared a position for the gun, where there was a fairly good field of fire. It was too dark to make out our position and no star-shells indicated the contour of the line. Where the enemy lay was a problem I could not solve.

Shorty came to where I was stationed.

"Want any biscuits and chocolate?" he asked.

"Why?" I queried, in some surprise.

"Come up here with me."

He took me to a dugout on the other side of the road and I saw that it had been a canteen which had been abandoned in a hurry. Boxes of chocolate and packets of biscuits were scattered about and I helped myself to sufficient for the other gunners.

"We might want these before we get away from here," said Shorty.

"What do you think will happen in the morning?" I asked.

"Over they'll come in massed formation and there'll be such targets as you never dreamt of," replied Shorty.

"That sounds happy," I said. "How long are we sticking here if that's on the board?

"Keep your ears open for the retreat," he answered. "They won't expect us to hold this road for long. They'll prepare for him further back, where the new trenches are."

We reached the gun position and Shorty looked over.

"Can't see a damn thing; wonder where the hell his line is. 'A' Company is somewhere in front, but it's too perishin' dark to make anything out."

A knot of men came down the road. A German had given himself up and he was being pestered for souvenirs. He was clad in new clothes and equipment and was very pleased that he had reached our lines without injury.

"Lucky devil," said Shorty, "he's finished now, and we've got to wait for hell to play before we can move a foot. Now, where the hell did that come from?"

A burst of machine-gun bullets had whistled down the road.

"That gun isn't far away," I remarked.

"Must be overhead fire. Couldn't be anything else," said Shorty. "Right-o! I'm coming." This as the word was passed along for Corporal ——.

I continued looking over the top. I was thinking of the coming dawn. A barrage would herald it, and then the endless waves of attacking Germans bent on killing. I hated war and the thoughts of death, but I intended firing that gun as long as possible. I might not bear malice to any man who lay waiting over there in the darkness, but the hounds were out to kill and I was not going to be killed if I could find a way to avoid it. I tried to imagine what would happen. "A" and "B" Companies would retire on to the road. That much was certain. But would they get back quickly enough to give us the chance of opening out before the Germans got too close? If they did, and the gun was all right, we might get a dozen magazines off. That should clear the front that affected us, and if the others did the same, we should have a chance to retire when the order was given. But, I thought, supposing I keep firing and the Germans keep coming and the order to retire isn't given. Must I wait there until some German bayonets me at his leisure? I mentioned the point to the others.

"What are we going to do in that event?"

"Run—like hell," said one of the men.

"You get five years for running," I answered.

"And six foot of earth if you stop here," he replied.

"We ain't going to stop here to be killed like dogs," put in another gunner.

"No, from what I can see it will be a case of every man for himself, and the best thing to do if we find the attack is too strong, is to jump the road and get up the other bank. His barrage will have lifted and we shan't get trapped in the road."

"And what then?" they asked.

"Well, you get a better chance when a man has got to climb up a bank to you," I replied.

The moon had risen and the contour of the ground was clearly defined, but nothing could be distinguished to assure us of the position of the front companies, or of the enemy line.

"Pass the word for Lance-Corporal ——."

I pricked up my ears. What was on? I walked up the road and met an officer of another platoon,

"Bring your gun and detail two men to accompany you," he said.

I went back and returned with the Lewis and two gunners, who were not altogether pleased with the selection.

"We think there is a machine-gun lying on the right between us and 'B' Company," said the officer. "He has probably been overlooked and he's enfilading the road pretty badly." He paused and then added: "The captain wants you to go out and mop him up."

"Whereabouts is he?" I asked.

"We don't know, but his fire comes from there chiefly." He pointed in a certain direction.

I could see that I was being asked to embark on a risky adventure, walking about open ground in moonlight looking for a concealed machine-gun.

"Don't you think it would be better if the gun was left here? We might have a better chance of locating them without it," I suggested.

"I'm sorry," he replied, "the company officer's orders are that you are to mop up the Bosche, and that you are to take the gun. I shall bring a platoon along the road."

Nothing more could be said. I turned to the men who were coming with me.

"I'm a married man," said one.

"So am I," I replied. "Come on, let's go."

We climbed the bank of the sunken road and proceeded steadily in the direction that had been indicated. I expected that if we missed the machine-gunner we should come across one of the front companies and they might have more accurate information of the position of the German. What bothered me chiefly was that if it was correct that an enemy gunner lay between the lines he would have a tremendous advantage over us and could wait until we were within easy range before he opened fire. There was, however, a possibility of him firing down the sunken road and thus betraying his position before he could observe us, and we might then have a chance to creep close to him and put paid to his account.

We had walked a hundred yards and everything was so quiet that I began to think some mistake had occurred. Suddenly one of the men shouted, "Look out", and I was in the act of flinging myself on the ground when a single rifle blazed directly in front of me and I felt a sickening crash in the top part of my body.

"I'm hit," I cried.

"For Christ's sake shut up and let's get away," came the reply.

A machine-gun opened with a roar but a few yards away, and I instinctively clenched my teeth, expecting to be struck again.

I took a deep breath for I hardly knew where I was hit.

"Lungs all right," I thought, with a certain amount of satisfaction.

I commenced to crawl on my hands and knees, dragging the gun with me. My right arm and shoulder felt peculiar. A star-shell was fired and dropped on the ground very near, where it furiously blazed. I lay quite still and a volume of rifle and machine-gun bullets passed over me. The light burned out, and still on my hands and knees I crawled some distance, and then, getting up, ran almost on to the fixed bayonet of one of "D" Company's men.

"Hell!" he cried, "I thought you were a Jerry; what's happened?"

"I've stopped one," I replied; "where's the stretcher-bearers?"

"I'll take you," said he. "Come on, let's have your equipment off first."

He released the straps and it dropped in a heap, and on second thoughts I extracted the water-bottle. He led me to a dugout.

A score of the Black Watch of the 51st Division were sitting there. All that was left of a battalion, they told me.

The stretcher-bearer cut away my tunic and shirt.

"My word, you've got a beauty, right on the shoulder. You'll never carry a pack again," he remarked.

He put on a field-dressing.

"It will stick," he said, "you needn't bother about it."

My mind was somewhat confused. Getting shot is not an everyday occurrence. It inspires hope or fear, according to its location and intensity.

I knew that the blood trickling down my side had snapped the bonds which held me to war, and I felt curiously happy. I was free to depart when and where I liked. No longer did the dawn hold nameless terrors for me. I could walk unchallenged out of the trenches, for the sight of torn flesh was the open sesame to the rear.

I felt that I should like to stay and rest for a while, but they urged me to get away while it was quiet.

"He may come over any minute," said one of the Black Watch. "Best clear out while you've got the chance."

So I wished them good-bye, and mounted the steps of the dugout. Neither Shorty nor Tanky were within sight. The shot which had wounded me, and the subsequent firing, had sent the whole of the company scurrying up the sunken road. Not a soul was about, but I had been directed to follow the road until I came to a trench which would lead me a considerable distance to the rear. I found the trench and came across some men.

"Who are you?" I asked.

"Worcesters, 'A' Company," they replied.

A little further along I found "B" Company. I was amazed, but did not stay to converse. I wanted to get as far away as possible. If those companies were "A" and "B", then "D" Company must be facing the Germans, and I had nearly walked into the enemy front line.

I came to an advanced dressing-station, and many stretcher cases were lying on the ground about the dugout.

"Any chance of being dressed?" I asked.

"Who are you?"

"Worcester."

"We can't look after you. This is a Gloucester dressing station. Follow the right of the moon until you strike a sunken road. You will find the field ambulance there."

I went on alone. It was quiet. Not a shell was being fired; but I was feeling weak and my shoulder was numbed, and the blood was still trickling down my side so that my clothes were wet with it. I must find that field ambulance. And so I followed the right of the moon until I came to the sunken road, and could hear the throb of motor traffic—of motor ambulances. I turned and looked in the direction I had come. The sky was clear, but the ground in the distance was shrouded in darkness, and I knew that in that darkness men were waiting, waiting with awful impatience, the dawn of doom, and I seemed to see Shorty, towering over the trench, with grim set face and glaring eyes, murmuring incantations to the gun as he faced the German hordes.

CHAPTER XXVII

CONCLUSION

SIX months had elapsed. The war was nearing the end, much nearer than most people dared hope. I had passed through the various stages of hospital life and was now at a training depot on the south-east coast. My category was low, beautifully low, and I was not worried by the prospect of further contact with the trenches. The stripe which I had worn for a year no longer adorned my sleeves. That was but the playfulness of the army authorities, to award stripes in the field which counted as nil in England. As a kind of consolation prize, I had been given an armlet with the mystic letters "R.P." embossed thereon. Translated, it meant Regimental Police. It was not a thing of beauty, but it gave me the privilege and the authority to keep the dogs out of the camp, and also to discourage sundry evil-disposed persons from getting away with army blankets and other paraphernalia. For two spells of four hours each I adorned a well-worn sentry box which looked out on to the main street that skirted the camp, and for two spells of four hours each I ruminated on the perils of the past and the hopes of the future. The future was rosy, as all futures should be. I was not exactly out of the wood, but I was getting pretty near the edge. To-morrow, I go away to a transfer centre where discharges are as numerous as whizbangs round a trench-mortar. The prospect is alluring. I whistle contentedly and give the sentry box a friendly smack.

Along the road comes swaggering a well-built figure. I rub my eyes, and a couple of mongrels, real opportunists, slip into the sacred citadel unchallenged. It is Shorty. Shorty, a sergeant, with the ribbon of the Military Medal on his breast. He sees me and the well-known smile extends from ear to ear.

We shake hands with much warmth.

"Where did you find it?" I asked, indicating the ribbon.

"Soon after you left," he answered.

"And three stripes, too?" I continued. "Been doing well with the rations, haven't you?"

Shorty chuckled as he replied:

"Win 'em and wear 'em."

For a few minutes we talked over old times and I heard with pleasure that Tanky was recovering from a leg wound somewhere in England, and then Shorty passed up the road and out of my life.

. . . . . .

A decade has gone by and the war has been relegated to the limbo of history. The grass is growing green in the valleys of the Somme and on the fields of Flanders. In every town or village monuments to the dead bear silent testimony to the deeds of yesterday. What have we done? What have we learnt? Has this war to end all wars fulfilled its destiny? Have we who suffered nine-tenths of the slaughter moved to prevent its recurrence? Hark! Faintly the drums are rolling. Tattoos are intriguing.

Another generation that knows not war is springing up, and the filth of war is clothed in brightness and glamour, and invested with righteousness, until the day shall come which shall disclose its stark nakedness of horror and expose it in its welter of blood and dying men and desolated countries.

And the war lords of the world are plotting and brewing the hotch-potch, and the ingredients they are preparing are more potent, more poisonous, than anything yet attempted.

Nations are sitting tight, licking their wounds and squabbling over armoury.

There is one bright speck that could be developed to produce a lasting peace. It is the League of Nations. The strength of a League, backed by the united support of a continent of people, would be despotic. The man or men who would force war for personal ambition, or general conquest, or even pride of race, should be ruthlessly checked, and a powerful League could do. it But the time is now.

Too late, when the flag is flying and the flaming torch is carried through the length and breadth of the land; when the blood runs hot and a barrage of propaganda brings men rallying to the standard of liberty—the liberty that entails serfdom.

Too late, when those lines of men are standing to attention in Phœnix Park, or Regent's Park, or wherever men are congregated for warlike purposes, be they British, or American, or Continental, and the unhappy countries of Europe re-echo to the rhythm of martial music.

Too late, then. The sons of the slaves of the war lords will be marching to the sacrifice.

THE END

Printed in the United Kingdom
by Lightning Source UK Ltd.
134911UK00001B/2/A

9 781843 421368